THE CHURCH

THE CHURCH

✝

by

Giovanni Battista Cardinal Montini

HELICON

Baltimore — Dublin

260M

Helicon Press, Inc.
1120 N. Calvert Street
Baltimore, Maryland 21202

Library of Congress Catalog Card Number 64-14667

from the original Italian *Discorsi su la Chiesa*
edited by Ufficio Studi Arcivescovili di Milano

translated by Alfred Di Lascia

this translation published with the authorization of
the Ordinary of Montreal
March 19, 1964   No. 774

Printed in the United States of America by
Garamond/Pridemark Press, Baltimore, Maryland

Contents

PART ONE

THE ESSENTIAL ASPECTS OF THE CHURCH   11

The Church: The Way to the Father—Historical Aspect—Mystical Aspect—Hierarchical Aspect—The Parish—A Prayer

THE MISSION OF THE CHURCH   21

The Origin of the Church's Mission—Orthodoxy and the Mandate—Specific Ends—Consequences of the Apostolate —The Apostolic Vocation of the Layman—The Sphere of the Apostolate—Confronting the Contemporary World—The Testimony of Love

THE CHARITY OF THE CHURCH TOWARDS THE ALIENATED   49

The Church's Universalistic Program—The Problem of the "Alienated"—The Church's "Relativism"—The Necessity of the Pastoral Art—Pastoral Sensitivity—Not Criticism but Love—Pastoral Action

THE SECRET OF THE CATHEDRAL   69

The Charm of the Cathedral—The Cathedral Is an Expression of Unity—The Secret of the Cathedral Is Christ's Presence—We Must "Raise from the Dead" the Spirit of the Church

6 *The Church*

THE PAPACY AND UNITY IN THE CHURCH   81
The Concept of the Church's Unicity—The Fundamental
Idea of Unity—The Church's Fundamental Composition—
The Relations Between the Pope and the Church's Unity—
The Pope's Authority—To Construct Unity

WHAT THE CHURCH IS AND WHAT THE CHURCH IS NOT 103
We must Understand the Church Anew—Corrupt Aspects
That Fail to Define the Church's Reality—The Church Is
Not an Ancient, Conservative Institution—The Church
Does Not Teach an Aprioristic, Incomprehensible, Indisput-
able, Rigid Doctrine—The Church Is a Mystery—The
Divine and Human Countenance of the Church, Mystical
Body of Christ—To Call the Church "Mother" Is to Under-
stand It in a Fresh Way and Love It

PART TWO

ECUMENICAL COUNCILS IN THE LIFE OF THE CHURCH 129
Incalculable Importance of the Ecumenical Council—The
Concept of Ecumenical Council—The Function of the
Ecumenical Council—Expectations Surrounding the Forth-
coming Ecumenical Council

LET US THINK ABOUT THE COUNCIL   149
Importance of the Event—Why Is the Council in Rome?—
The Expectation of the Entire Christian Community—The
Primacy of Peter, the Church's Foundation—The Divine
Mystery of the Church, Christ's Mystical Body—The Con-
cept of the Reform of Christian Life—Some Concrete
Prospects—The Impact of the Council on Society and the
World—The Church and Its Universal Salvific Mission—
The Call of Charity and Unity to Our Separated Brothers—
The Dimensions of Our Concrete Commitment—"To Feel
with the Church and the Pope"

ECUMENICAL COUNCILS IN AN INTERNATIONAL
HISTORICAL FRAMEWORK 193

The Importance of an Historical Event and Its Impact on
the World—The Relations between the Council and Civil
Society—The Autonomy of Powers Affirmed by St.
Ambrose and St. Charles—The Unconcern of Secular
Society Involves an Incomprehension of the Divine Mystery
—The Church's Call to the World—The Council and Its
Relations with the Contemporary World

COUNCILS IN THE LIFE OF THE CHURCH 213

Necessity of Studying Some of the Council's Prospects—We
Should Deepen the Concept of "Church"—The Church's
Social Constitution—The Characteristic Notes of the Church
Expressed by a Council—A Council Gives the Church's
Countenance a Full and Radiant Expression—A Glance at
Past Councils—What Significance Will Vatican Council II
Have?

PART ONE

The Essential Aspects of the Church

Some people have the idea that as religion is worked out in concrete forms ever closer to our own experience, it becomes mixed and tarnished with earthly elements. So it is that some will experience more difficulty in hearing us speak of the Church our Mother than of God our Father. For whatever takes on an earthly form, having once been heavenly, may well exhibit traits that are less beautiful and less pure, enmeshed in matter as they have indeed become.

Yet we must note two things. The first is that our religion is true, positive and real. It does not harbor vague, imprecise truths, nor does it rest on dogmas that are mutable and not at all coercive. Our religion is not pure sentimentality; it is rather a relationship with God such as he has willed and established. If God has willed the incarnation (that is, the assumption of human flesh into divine life) and if he has willed the redemption (that is, the great drama of the passion and expiating death for that very evil which has called forth this two-fold action in Christ), it is a sign that he has chosen and sublimated our flesh and our history in order to reveal himself and communicate with both men and the Church. Indeed, the Church is nothing but the continuation of Christ and the meeting-point, in the movement of history,

11

between God and men. It is not in heaven that God has fixed this meeting-point but here on earth among men—that is, in Christ. He has not fixed a meeting-point that is private for each person but one which is socially organized, namely the Church, where each person may find him and therein communicate with him. The second point to note is that the Church presents two aspects: the one, external, may seem to be worn and tarnished by time and earth and hence subject to defect and misery; the other, internal, is all holy and sanctifying, divine and resplendent.

Those outside the Church will suffer occasionally from its human imperfections, although if they view it with a serene eye they will recognize many marvellous things even in the temporal phases of this great ship of salvation. But those who enter the Church will weep with joy, for they will see in it the very beautiful and holy spouse of Christ, our mother and our teacher; they will see humanity transfigured and rejoice in the knowledge that the Church was waiting, all this time, just for them, as a mother awaits a child long away, and rejoices—as the child itself does—upon its return.

The Church: The Way to the Father

It is impossible to exhaust all aspects of ecclesiology in one meditation. Our aim is rather to stress a single aspect. Since it is only within the Church that an encounter with our Father is possible, we should like to call attention to the social, community aspect of genuine christian piety in the face of the individualism that is so pervasive, especially in our cities and even among men of good will.

We should also like to clarify an understanding and appreciation of the true nature of the hierarchical structure of the Church which many tend to consider an intrusion between the soul and God. We shall end with a reference to the communion of saints, and lift up our wondering thought to Mary most holy, mother of Christ, our most blessed mother and *typus Ecclesiae.*

We may begin by commenting on the following three passages: "the Son of God, who loved me, and gave himself for me" (Gal 2:20); ". . . Jesus Christ, who died, nay, has risen again, and sits at the right hand of God, is pleading for us? Who will separate us from the love of Christ? Will affliction, or distress, or persecution, or hunger, or nakedness, or peril, or the sword? For thy sake, says the scripture, we face death at every moment, reckoned no better than sheep marked down for slaughter. Yet in all this we are conquerors, through him who has granted us his love" (Rom 8:34-37); "Christ shewed love to the Church when he gave himself up on its behalf" (Eph 5:25).

In his wisdom God has willed that each one of us receive the gifts of his love through the community, perhaps because it is only within the community that the whole range of potential human (and christian) greatness may be fulfilled, and because any kind of isolation is both an impoverishment and a weakness. As this occurs on the human plane so does it on the supernatural, that is, the plane of God's paternal love. For God loves me and each and every one of us in particular but has willed that I, indeed each one of us, become united with him through a brotherly union of one with all. Such is the very reason for the existence of the Church.

The Church: Historical Aspect

In the Old Testament God chose a people who had followed him in a special way through law, direct intervention and special revelation. It was "his people" who maintained his worship, memory and love on earth, and in whom the history of the salvation of the whole of mankind was initiated and actualized (cf. Ex 19: 4-6, etc.). Christ's advent within the bosom of the chosen people has widened the boundaries for all who cleave to him through faith and grace.

God's new people is made up of God's children, of us christians united with Christ risen and forever living (Mt 8: 11; 28: 8-20). Since that time, as a mustard seed (Mt 13: 31), the Church has grown into a magnificent tree and spread its roots and branches throughout the entire earth.

The Church: Mystical Aspect

Too many people look at the Church in its external forms alone: its organization; its cohesiveness in doctrine and morality; the fruits of perfection and holiness—and of martyrdom in every century—in those who accept it completely; its marvellous twenty centuries of history; its uninterrupted existence without the aid of human forces and despite the sins of its members, and even on occasion of its hierarchy; its charity; its revolutionary impact on the world and on different civilizations. . . .

Now, what animates and sustains all of this? To what end is it all directed? Where can we find an explanation of the Church's strength? We are greatly interested in answering this question because for a Catholic christian nothing is more necessary and vital than the Church whence he receives all that he has. We do not make ourselves Catholic all alone, in isolation; it is the Church that joins us to Christ and presents itself as a reality that exists long before we do, and is greater than we are. It is not we who make the Church: it is rather the Church that makes us Catholics. Truth, grace, the sacraments: all the certain norms for our journey to God come from the Church. The Church is not only a visible society endowed with religious ends; it is likewise a mystery, for its head is the same Christ who lived twenty centuries ago and still lives today because he has risen. Christ has no successors: only visible representatives. The

strength, truth and holiness of the Father circulate throughout the Church, and it is always in and through the Church
that we see the action of Christ, man and God, communicat-
ing the Father's life to mankind.

Let us call attention to the analogy of the body (Eph 1:
22ff; Col 2: 19) and of the living temple (Eph 2: 19-22),
and insist on the dynamic aspect of the two images in so far
as they present the Church as experiencing an uninterrupted
growth in which each one of us and of our brethren becomes involved.

The Church: Hierarchical Aspect

Let us begin with the image of the body as it is advanced in
Romans 12: 4-16 or 1 Corinthians 4: 30, and we shall learn
that the Church is not made up of homogeneous elements
(as a mineral), but of elements that are different one from
the other, as in every living organism. If we think of the
distribution of different offices and powers we shall understand the necessity for a hierarchy. For as in a body there
is a brain and a heart with related systems, so in the Church
there is a hierarchy commissioned to teach, direct and dis-
tribute the sacraments, that is, the means of grace. It is clear
from the gospel that, out of a great many disciples, Jesus
chose twelve and assigned them special tasks under one sole
head (Mt 10: 16, 18ff, etc.).

In the passage cited above, St. Paul mentions other gifts
and special vocations that God bestows even upon those
who are not members of the hierarchy: the gift of alms-
giving, of knowing how to comfort those who suffer, of
deepening sacred knowledge. . . . Even the extraordinary
mission to perform miracles and the gift of private revelation
enter into this category (cf. the passage in 1 Cor). Both the
vocation of the hierarchy and the special gifts are granted for
the welfare of all, that is, the communitarian good; hence it

would be as absurd to boast of the gifts we do have as it would be naive to envy those we do not.

Certainly the hierarchy must not be tolerated as an intrusion between ourselves and God, for it is precisely the hierarchy that, by virtue of its sacred mission, guarantees our union with the Father through Jesus Christ.

In conclusion, let us acknowledge the fact that it is by living together in the society of saints (that is, the Church) that we become united with God and receive a vast number of benefits. Let us not alienate ourselves from the Church nor believe that we can do better by ourselves. This would be an illusion, as it is indeed the error of individualism carried over into religion.

As we receive, so must we give to the community, to the Church. Let each one of us examine his own talents, his own powers, his own secret impulses given by the Holy Spirit, and let each one of us decide how he can use those powers most fruitfully, not just for himself but for the good of everybody.

Let us above all love the Church. It is in the Church that we find ourselves flanked and sustained by our brothers, each for all and all for each, and it is also in the Church that we especially find our mother, Mary most holy. For not only is Mary that most beautiful historical figure who has given us Jesus once and for all, but she is the mother who continues to influence the spiritual development of her children, just as a mother on earth influences the creature still enclosed within her womb. Without Mary the Church could easily seem like an impersonal and cold organism; instead Mary is there in the Church, as the mother who knows and loves us and is never absent from the inmost drama of the least of her children.

Meditation on the profound reality of the Church must lead at least to an initial vision of the Church as a continuation of Christ. This is "his church," his sphere of action, the "place" where he acts through the Holy Spirit. It is Christ Jesus who never abandons us, who communicates his life, teaching, doctrine and love, who redeems and prepares us for the meeting with our Father.

The Parish

It is by the will of Christ that there is a hierarchy in the Church to guarantee our personal union with God, and it is also by Christ's will that there are laymen entrusted with missions and duties of their own which they should carry out without allowing the hierarchy to act in their stead. On the whole it is through the parish, through a small part of the Church, that we come in contact with the Church itself. And as the great Church, so the parish must be a community of persons, a family that bears witness to and foreshadows the heavenly community of the blessed.

All must know one another, for all are children of the one Father, on their journey to his home. All must love one another, for such is Christ's command and the christian's task: to continue on earth, in so far as possible, the love with which the Father loves both Christ and us. All must pray together, especially in offering the sacrifice of Jesus. Sunday Mass is no time for individual prayer, for novenas or tridua, or for the lighting of candles. Jesus is present in the midst of his brethren and offers himself with us who offer him to the Father and who, together with him, offer the sorrow, the labor, the fruit, the hope of each and every one of us: *cor unum et anima una.* All must have something to do and not simply stand by passively, for the parish belongs neither to the pastor nor his assistants, nor are they the parish: activity, industry, good example, interest, attendance, order, cleanliness, spiritual and material progress, church ornaments and furnishing, catechetical teaching . . . all of these constitute the right and duty of each and every parishioner.

Why so many absences and then . . . so many criticisms?

A Prayer

"I came upon an errand from my Father, and now I am sending you out in my turn . . . he who listens to you, listens to me" (Jn 20: 21; Lk 10: 16), said Jesus to his Apostles and their successors. Lord Jesus, teach us how we may see and hear you in your Church!

Lord Jesus, make us the devout faithful of your Church!

Nobody can reach the Father except through your Church, O Jesus, because you have so willed. It is only through living in the Church, through heeding its teachings, through sharing in its prayers and sacraments and obeying its laws that we can be sure of finding God.

Lord Jesus, make us the devout faithful of your Church!

Even under the human countenance of your Church we find your divine countenance, O Jesus, we find you! It is you who live in the Church, you who rule it, you who direct and sustain it throughout the centuries.

Lord Jesus, make us the devout faithful of your Church!

Within your Church, O Lord, we are all present and united. With us are all the saints of all the ages, with us is Mary most holy, your mother and our mother. Never are we alone!

Lord Jesus, make us worthy of our saints!

United with Christ who unites us among ourselves, let us all pray together:

Our Father . . .

Lord Jesus, guide us to the Father, within your Church!

Make of all christians one single body enlivened by your spirit!

Lord, God omnipotent and our Father, nobody can reach

you except through the Church of Jesus. Grant us who are already within the Church the power to become living and active members, to believe in the Church's teaching, to carry out its instructions, rules, teachings, and give ourselves to its service so that we may live as true children of yours.

Through Christ our Lord. Amen.

The Mission
of the Church

Why, my friends, do you ask me to speak to you about what you already know? Is not the mission of the Church already known to you through faith, knowledge and experience? What can I add to the well known words of Christ, who defines the mission of the Church in the fateful words to his apostles: "You, therefore, must go out, making disciples of all nations, and baptizing them in the name of the Father, and of the Son, and of the Holy Spirit, teaching them to observe all the commandments which I have given you" (Mt 28: 19-20)? Or do you perhaps wish to hear those well known and beloved words repeated so that you may enjoy their prophetic sound and experience their historical reality, admire their simplicity and majesty, feel them alive and operative within you, even today?

Do you wish to hear them as if they were new, as if they had been freshly uttered, so that you may experience with an inner palpitation of your heart the secret power which transforms the fisherman into an apostle, the disciple into a teacher, and the timid follower into an heroic witness? Again, do you wish to hear these words so that you may meditate on how it is that they have been addressed precisely to you through a simple yet most paradoxical combination

21

of factors? For among thousands and thousands of men on this earth and among thousands and thousands of adherents to the religion of Christ, it is you, precisely you, who in some way and in some measure are called to the great and mysterious mission.

Do you wish to hear that the mission of the Church is your mission, too? Do you wish, for a moment, to transform this Congress into an examination of conscience, into a meditation which might at one and the same time lift and comfort and penetrate your soul? And might not these words create within the inner recesses of your soul a new consciousness and a fresh force as if the evangelical voice, as mild as it is strong, and as authoritative as it is friendly, were to echo from within—"The Master is here, and bids thee come" (Jn 11: 28)?

Do you perhaps wish to hear this well known doctrine again, so that you may honor the bearer, not indeed in his person but in his ministry? Is it in this way that you really wish to experience the value, the depth, the beauty and effectiveness of this teaching, and to receive it in living humility not merely as a speculative doctrine but as a living communication from those who, by divine mandate, are obliged to transmit it as they themselves have received it, from apostle and bishop?

Once again, do you realize that, in inviting me to talk to you about the mission of the Church, it is our precise duty to reflect so that we may gain a better understanding of what, in the long run, the Church actually is? For us, the Church has been an education that has gone almost unnoticed, so natural has it been to us. But now we must transform it into our own knowledge and life. From a heritage of the past, it must become a treasure for the present; and from a tradition, it must become a consciousness and a vital force. Do you realize that in deepening our knowledge of the Church's doctrine we succeed in discovering its divine originality, the secret of its eternal youth, the fascination of its beauty, the principle of its inexhaustible fecundity? Do you realize that reflection on the mystery of the Church has become the central question around which revolves not only the study of modern theology but the religious spirit of our generation? And do you know that in this is to be found the mark of its orthodoxy, the source of its prayer, the hope of its spiritual conquest of both the contemporary world and of the world of the future?

If such is the case, it is not fruitless for us to listen again to the ancient and living lesson on the mission of the Church. This lesson is entirely contained in one simple proposition: the mission of the Church is the continuation of Christ.

Remember what the Vatican Council teaches us: "The Eternal Pastor and Bishop of our souls, in order to continue for all time the life-giving work of his redemption, decided to build the Church wherein, as in the house of the living God, all who believe might be united in the bond of one faith and one charity."[1] You might also wish to remember what the pope teaches us in the Encyclical on the Mystical Body: "Just as in fact the Word of God willed to make use of our nature in order to redeem man, burdened by sorrow and torment, so almost in the same fashion does he make use of his Church throughout the ages, for the purpose of continuing for all time the work already begun."[2]

We find ourselves faced with a fact which exhibits, at one and the same time, a two-fold aspect. First, we find identity, preservation, consistency, communion of life, loyalty, presence—that is, the Church as it is symbolized by the stability of a rock. Second, we find movement, communication, projection in time and space, expansion, dynamism, escatological hope—this is the Church as it is symbolized by the moving, living and growing body of Christ.

1. Heinrich Denzinger, *Enchiridion Symbolorum*, 1821.
2. *A.A.S.*, 1943, 199.

The mission of the Church invites us to consider the trajectory of Christ in time, for it is that very trajectory that creates history, whose meaning and value can be communicated solely within human history. Indeed it can be sought and discovered nowhere else but in history.

While the word "mission" limits the immense range of the Church's doctrine, it summons us to contemplate the image of movement which marks the life of the Church and originates with Christ, who continues to inspire, promote and accompany it. As Christ is borne by the movement, he preaches and communicates, reaches men, surmounts the boundaries of nations, soars over centuries, and joins with human life in its manifold forms, institutions, customs and civilizations. The living movement of the Church suffers opposition and persecution. It finds many who are faithful, experiences victory and triumph. It continues to suffer and grow, to pray, work, help, teach. The movement of the Church continues on toward an end which at one and the same time attracts it as though nearby and sustains it so firmly that it experiences neither weariness nor disappointment. The Church moves on in the hope that it will find fulfillment in a final day in which the mysterious Christ whom it bears will reveal himself to it, absorb it within himself and beatify it. This final day is life eternal.

This mission may therefore be compared to a journey in which the Church lives and grows and continues the work of redemption. Though it bears all the marks of a great and manifest human event, it is not simply an ordinary human event. The mission is a kind of continuous incarnation of Christ and hence originates in, lives and moves towards a mystery that is precisely Christ's inward presence. Whoever has formulated the theme of your Congress has rightly felt the need of bringing together the words "mission" and "mystery."

The Church's mission arises, acts and advances by virtue

of the mystery that generates, enlivens and prepares it for the final eschatological consummation. Jesus Christ has already traced the plot of his earthly life: "I have come forth from the Father into the world; and again I shall leave the world and go to the Father" (cf. Jn 16: 18). Similarly the Church may say of itself: I have sprung from Christ and I journey through the world, living my life through him; and to him I shall finally return. Thus the Church sketches the causes and the outline of its mysterious mission.

The Origin of the Church's Mission

Let us now inquire into the origin of the Church's mission and ask how it began not only in time but as the efficient and enduring principle of its authenticity, authority and vitality.

The mission finds its origin in Christ, as we were saying, but this is not the time for us to engage in a theological lecture. It is enough for us to remember that Christ is the founder of the Church and that it is he who institutes, engenders and sends it forth. We are all very familiar with the symbolic interpretation that the Church Fathers gave to the wound that gushed forth blood and water from the side of Christ crucified. Just as out of the rib of a sleeping Adam God drew Eve, mother of all the living, so out of Christ's rib, out of Christ who died for us on the cross, has come the Church, mother of all believers.[3]

We must therefore understand very well how Christ's mission becomes transformed into the Church's mission, for exactly in this lies the act whereby the Church comes into being, and in this lies its efficient cause. Above all, we should be interested in discovering and evaluating the apostolic nature of the Church, for in doing so we shall gain a deeper understanding of its hierarchical organization.

3. Cf. St. Augustine, *Tract.*, 120; Denzinger, 480.

Before leaving us he willed that there should always be in our
midst men invested with divine powers such that the action he
initiates from heaven may be conveyed to each one of us in a
sensible form and continue to affect us in a manner that is connatural to us, in the manner, that is, of a direct contact. We are
speaking of the hierarchical powers that, far from being a substitute
for Christ's action, are in fact subordinated to it so as to carry it,
in some way, through time and space.[4]

One of the essential points of Catholicism consists precisely
in this fact, that the Church's mission is derived from, indeed
is one with, Christ's mission.

Let us remember, in passing, what Jesus has said: "He
who listens to you, listens to me, he who despises you, despises me; and he who despises me, despises him that sent
me" (Lk 10: 16); and let us also remember what he added,
on the day of his resurrection: "I came upon an errand from
my Father, and now I am sending you out in my turn" (Jn
20: 21). We all know that this doctrine is basic, for it concerns Christ's awareness of his own mission and of its continuation on both the human and historical plane. It is
therefore no surprise that this doctrine has been subjected
to a very subtle and sophistical criticism as well as a very
rash and mistaken accusation.

But the truth is clear, as the whole of apostolic history
bears witness. The title that St. Paul claims as his own, "by
God's will an apostle of Jesus Christ" (2 Cor 1: 1), is more
than a personal vocation, more than a simple service, more
than a gratuitous and personal charism of the spirit: it is a
special mandate, an exceptional investiture that endows his
mission with an authenticity that is derived from and conferred by Christ: "an apostle not holding his commission
from men, not appointed by man's means, but by Jesus
Christ, and God the Father who raised him from the dead"
(Gal 1: 1). The Apostle thus appears at one and the same

4. Charles Journet, *The Church of the Word Incarnate* (New York:
Sheed and Ward, 1955), I, p. 9.

time as the principle of the continuity and expansion of christian revelation and of both the unity and authority of the community of believers that is arising around him. Early christianity is neither a tradition without authority nor a written law without a living guardian and interpreter. It is born of Christ, social and hierarchical, and is centered in the men who have received the mandate to establish, organize, teach and govern the nascent communities.[5]

All that we have just said has always constituted and continues to constitute for us a clear triumph over any other kind of exegesis, and in fact expresses the fundamental principles of the Church's mission.

Orthodoxy and the Mandate

Let us for a moment consider the nature of this fundamental principle which is characterized, as we were saying, by the identity of Christ's mission with that of the Church and by the passage of that identity from Christ to the Church; that is, by the apostle's mandate to extend, guarantee and carry out Christ's mission. And let us now identify and name these two fundamental traits so that we may both understand and participate in the Church's mission. They are orthodoxy and the mandate.

Orthodoxy, that is, the perfect derivation of the Church's mission from its true source, the jealous preservation of Christ's doctrinal and sacramental patrimony, the *depositum* that, as St. Paul teaches, every minister of the Gospel must faithfully preserve (1 Tim 6: 20), seems to check the mission in the very act in which it is about to get under way. It seems to bind it to an immovable, inflexible, alien and coercive principle that deprives the missionary of his freedom of thought and action, and mortifies his very personality.

Our modern individualism is not particularly sympathetic

5. Cf. Msgr. Battifol, *L'Eglise naissante,* p. 11.

to a form of thought and life that is defined once and for all,
and by the method of authority at that. The very religious
feeling of us modern men seems to become impoverished the
moment we feel obliged to fashion our lives after immutable
dogmas. Our religious fervor seems to die out the moment
we feel incapable of following the spontaneous impulses of
our feelings or of making use of our own uncoerced experiences. Many men and women are engaged in propagating
moral and religious ideas free of any obedience to Catholic
orthodoxy. At times they seem to be especially successful
in their actions and to win out in their arguments precisely
because they do not start from any fixed point, and are not
bound by any definite dogmas. They do not bear the burden,
sublime though heavy, of divine truths. The action of these
men and women springs from the genius and fanciful imagination of their spirit, that is frequently both generous and
sincere. Strengthened by some precious fragment of natural
morality, by some remembered biblical or philosophical passage, by some poetic and artistic inspiration or even by some
vague christian principle, these people dedicate themselves to
preaching the conversion of the world. They are apostles
acting under their own auspices, for they have no other truth
to proclaim than what is commensurate to their own human
capabilities. They lack the "mystery" that must move and
inform every genuine mission of salvation and hence lack
the true Christ, the living God. Their mission is no longer
religious, but human; no longer a continuation of Christ,
but simply a human affair.

We on the other hand must be absolutely convinced that
the mission of Christ entrusted to the Church is a matter of
the strictest orthodoxy. This mission is the bond that unites
us, the channel through which we communicate, the guarantee by which we are not only united with Christ but may
also experience his presence and his authority. It is indeed
an indispensable condition for receiving the divine heritage

and a guarantee of its being preserved intact. It makes us understand how the Church's mission is really a transmission of transcendent values, and how for that very reason it demands that those who carry out the mission should become conscious that they are disciples before being teachers, ministers before being defenders of the faith; in short, they should remember that they are a channel and not the fountainhead.

If Christ the teacher went so far as to say of himself, "And this word, which you have been hearing from me, comes not from me, but from my Father who sent me" (Jn 14: 24) what must those who wish to become his followers and missionaries say in order that they might be believed? We must form an idea of orthodoxy that is different from the prevailing one which construes orthodoxy as a kind of game for those who endure it and as a kind of whip for those who practice it. On the contrary, for us orthodoxy must consist in a passion for the truth that Christ has revealed and the Church teaches; a test of our wisdom and of our humility as these virtues dispose us to receive and communicate God's higher gifts; a certainty for our minds that must be based on the rock of divine truth rather than on the shifting sands of either human opinion or arbitrary eclecticism. Orthodoxy must furnish a stimulus for research and for action towards error. Finally, orthodoxy must mean that we should love rather than profess to win over through polemical arguments those whom we wish to save through the christian economy.

And at the same time as we discuss orthodoxy, let us also discuss the mandate.

Orthodoxy has to do with the substance of the heritage to be transmitted while the mandate has to do with the ability to transmit it; whereas the first element in the Church's mission is static, the second is dynamic.

The mission neither arises nor organizes itself on its own; it is rather the subject of a command and of an initial power that are to continue and to be transmitted in specific forms through the sacrament of orders and ecclesiastical jurisdiction. This is a magnificent doctrine that hardly needs comment except for the observation that nobody can become an apostle suddenly and through his own powers, for he must receive the mandate before he can carry out such a sublime function. And though it is true that all may and should join in the apostolic action of God's Church both through the power that baptism bestows upon every christian to share in the divine gifts and divine worship and through the *regale sacerdotium* conferred upon every believer, nevertheless this action is marked by a discipline that demands the most exact mandate in those who have been entrusted with protecting and promoting it for the very reason that it affects the sanctification and guidance of the clergy and of every single layman. This means, in effect, that those who wish to do apostolic work must depend on ecclesiastical authority rather than act entirely on their own, must join forces rather than go their separate ways, and offer their services rather than assert their freedom. They must feel themselves one not only with the interests of the Church but with its concrete visible structure. The apostolate is one disciplined army, one great act of cooperation rather than an exercise in freedom; the more it allows itself to be imbued with the hierarchical and communitarian spirit and the closer it moves towards those whom "the Holy Spirit has made bishops; you are to be the shepherds" (Acts 20: 28), the more perfect will it become.

Specific Ends

Now that we have traced the sources of the Church's mission we must see in what exactly it consists and what its specific and immediate ends may be. In this respect too we must begin with Christ and call to mind how he himself defines his mission.

At a moment that demanded just such a concise definition, in confronting Pilate, Jesus said: "What I came into the world for, is to bear witness of the truth" (Jn 18: 37). On another occasion in his public life he says: "That is what the Son of Man has come for, to search out and to save what was lost" (Lk 19: 10). As a child in the temple, sought by Mary, he replies: ". . . I must needs be in the place which belongs to my Father" (Lk 2: 49). All of this is summed up in our profession of faith as it is engraved in the Nicene Creed: for us men and our salvation he descended from heaven, was incarnate by the Holy Spirit from the Virgin Mary, was made man, suffered, was buried and rose from the dead.[6]

If the apostle's (that is, the Church's) mission is one with Christ's, we must clarify for ourselves with the utmost precision the nature and purpose of Christ's mission. For this too is a fundamental point, not only for theology but for our modern Catholic consciousness as well.

In recent years, as we all know, the christian event has been the object of criticism that has been extremely sharp and, on the whole, devastating. But since it is impossible to deny that christianity is a real and still operative event, the most diverse interpretations have been entertained in an effort to deny its supernatural prerogatives, contest its original character, and minimize its importance. This has been done to show clearly that some aspects of the christian event are but parts of a larger whole so as to use them for partisan purposes. This distortion of christianity at times assumes an attractive guise for the practical purposes intended and is even capable of seducing those of us who are believers.

It is common knowledge that Christ's mission, and hence the Church's mission that continues it, is related to the idea of salvation, that is, of a change in human conditions for the better.

6. Cf. Denzinger, p. 86.

But what kind of salvation? What kind of change? And how are these to be attained?

We say that the salvation which Christ brings is God's kingdom, that is, his religion, the relations which he has established between the heavenly Father and mankind, along with the whole range of conditions demanded by this relationship and all the consequences thereby entailed.

The Church's mission is essentially religious. It is neither directly political nor social nor economic, for it has to do with man in respect to his supreme end; it specifies and realizes his radical orientation toward God and proclaims his unmerited yet most joyful supernatural elevation to sonship with God. And so it is that divine truth enters into our life and seeks to be accepted in virtue of the source whence it springs, the very word of God. It is the good tidings, the Gospel that interprets the world as seen by God and invites mankind to judge both itself and the world in this light, at once joyful and bitter. It is a free and wonderful encounter in time and space between two woefully unequal wills, the will of God with its rigorous demand for love and the will of man who determines his eternal destiny through the kind of response he makes.

The christian mission is a redemption effected by Christ as priest and victim of a sacrifice that is capable of absorbing and cancelling all the debts that sinning mankind is unable to settle, that is capable of bringing the same mankind to a new birth in innocence; it is a communion of life and powers that Christ has transmitted to his followers. Finally, it is the christian mission that creates here on earth a particular and perfect society called the Church and prepares the way for the final union between Christ and his mystical body, beyond the boundaries of the world and of present history.

Thus the christian mission is neither a simple statement of a few principles which the philosophical evolution of human thought can make its own, nor is it a vague spiritualism designed either to intoxicate our emotions or narcotize our suffering. It is neither a lyrical prophetism nor a charismatic mysticism designed to arouse obscure and superstitious energies within the inner depths of our imagination and instincts; nor is it a naturalistic humanism directly aimed at benefiting the temporal order. Much less is the christian mission a revolution that might wish to correct social injustices by inciting one class against another. Neither should the christian mission be understood as adopting an apathetic and resigned attitude in the face of the world as it is, nor as calmly awaiting a future rebirth in which everything will finally be set aright.

The christian mission is very original indeed and very demanding, and is easier to practice than to define. The Church's mission consists in extending Christ's life throughout the world and in helping mankind to participate in his mysteries, the incarnation and the redemption. The Church's mission therefore is to establish a communion of life with him and, consequently, a communion of brotherhood among all. The Church's mission is to give birth to the Church itself, to bring it to life, to help it spread and bear fruit in the works of faith, grace and the Gospel. As a living tree, the Church produces itself, brings forth its own branches and ripens its own fruit. "I am the vine, you are its branches," Jesus says (Jn 15: 5).

Consequences of the Apostolate

If we understand the nature of the Church's mission well we shall be in a position to draw some consequences of the utmost importance for developing an apostolic mentality. The first consequence is this: the Church bears within itself the immediate purpose of its own mission for it is, in a certain sense, its own end. The Church serves no other end than what is immanent in the affirmation of its own life; in fact there exists no end that is higher or more necessary than its own. This is the conception of the Church's mission that justifies its independence of the state and of all other human enterprises and interests. The Church is free because it is self-sufficient in virtue of its constitution. Furthermore, the Church is its own end and must work directly for itself, but not in order to achieve an egotistic self-sufficiency nor in order to restrict man's goodness and activity. It must work because it bears a unique form of life, supreme and integral, in which the temporal and human forms of life may find nourishment not as instruments pressed into its service but rather as principles working for its own good. "Make it your first care to find the kingdom of God," the Divine Master teaches (Mt 6: 33).

This primacy in the Church's mission of God's kingdom (that consists in preaching the Gospel) has, as every one knows, been the object of debate even among Catholics. These have been lively and, recently, marked by some incidents that have been spiritually dramatic in character. The attempt to give the work of human and social redemption priority over the work of moral and religious redemption has been expressed in achievements that have been as significant as they have been unfortunate. Nor have any merely pragmatic reasons prompted this humanistic effort, made in the light of human charity, to initiate the missionary and pastoral work that properly pertains to the Church. No, it is rather a matter of principle that involves a preference of temporal over spiritual needs, of human over supernatural means, of economic over religious redemption, of social over moral reform. You all know that Catholic evangelization aims first of all at engendering faith even though, in order to accomplish this, it must employ the means of charity. There are others, however, who believe that preaching a definitive and binding faith is of secondary importance, and that rather it is desirable that some people should propagate certain moral precepts on grounds called—heaven alone knows why—absolute, while others should perform works of charity and engage in education.

You also know that some of us unfortunately have strayed from the right path, almost out of distress and excess of zeal.

In the light of the present conditions that make it difficult to christianize the working class, christians are urged to act in two successive stages: first liberation, and only after that evangelization. The first of the two stages is independent of christian norms. . . . There is but one true attitude for us to adopt, and that is to remain silent, silent for a long time, silent for years, and to participate in the whole life, the whole struggle, the whole culture latent in our working population which we have often unwittingly deceived. At the same time we have also renounced all intention of converting.[7]

For this is no longer the Church's mission.

We must also note that the Church's mission is to expand, even though it finds within itself, as does every living organism, the proximate reasons for its activities. Its mission is to expand because the Church itself is a diffusion of Christ, a communication of grace and powers, a participation in Christ's priesthood. Furthermore, such a mission is the fruit of the Church's charity, the vehicle for the Holy Spirit, the fulfillment of God's plan, the object of Christ's prayer.

The work of salvation conceived by God is one and Catholic, and runs its course according to the one divine plan that bears Christ at its center. Unity is already given, already exists in the world. The one true Church already exists and so does the one legitimate succession to the fullness of Christ, in the form known as the vicariate, that is, the papacy. The

7. Montuclard as quoted in Léon-Joseph Cardinal Suenens, *The Church in a Missionary State*, p. 28f.

plan extends to the whole of mankind and widens out till it reaches a universal and catholic range which, though existing by right, has yet to exist completely in fact. In order actually to achieve universality God has willed to use Christ's humanity as well as his ministry which he has created. Assisted by the free and rightful cooperation of all believers, God has also willed to use particular men both as instruments for carrying out the sacramental faculty of orders and as secondary causes in discharging jurisdictional powers. God has willed that men should take part in bringing about their salvation. "We are God's helpers," St. Paul says (1 Cor 3: 9). This is the sense in which it is said that "God needs men." Through the apostolate unity stretches out to become the Catholic world, and through the apostolate the Catholic world flows into a unity. Such is the dynamism proper to the Church's mission, as this in turn is a continuation of Christ's mission.

The Apostolic Vocation of the Layman

Though you must have meditated on these truths many times before, it is only now that you attend to them so that you may experience their powerful fascination and feel their irresistible force. It is not my purpose to illustrate more exactly how and why a certain apostolic investiture may also be communicated to laymen; I would rather remind you how and why today a true apostolic vocation does resound in their souls.

Truth is by nature universal. Truth is Christ's message. Those who possess truth possess light, both for themselves and for others, and those who esteem the value of light love to spread about its beneficial rays.

And what if truth were necessary for life? As necessary as bread, for me and others; as necessary as a raft that brings salvation in the midst of the universal shipwreck of mankind.

"He who believes and is baptized will be saved, he who refuses belief will be condemned" (Mk 16: 16). And why should some men perish for a failure that is due far more to those who have failed to give them their means of salvation than it is to their own ignorance? If some should fail to receive the life-giving truth because of our egotism and culpable negligence, who would be judged more severely: those who have received the gift of faith and have failed to share it with their fellow men, or those who have received no such gift because there were no apostles to communicate it to them?

Truth and faith—that is, the truth necessary for salvation —engender a responsibility in those who possess it (cf. Mt 11: 20ff). We must not put our lamp under a bushel measure (cf. Mt 5: 15). Though our responsibility is in fact great and pressing it is not to be hated, for it is born of a loving design that obliges us to carry it out in and through love. It is love that drives us (cf. 2 Cor 5: 14). Though all believers should, to a certain extent, feel an impulse to become apostles as a law of faith and grace, yet the impulse is felt most strongly by those souls that, through either an internal or external calling, are given the impulse to serve truth and bear witness. A higher and unconditional obligation makes the impulse irrepressible: "It is impossible for us to refrain from speaking of what we have seen and heard . . . we are witnesses; we and the Holy Spirit God gives to all those who obey him (Acts 4: 20; 5: 32).

Today we find ourselves in the presence of the historical and spiritual phenomenon; indeed we are, in a certain sense, the protagonists. The need to bear witness does affect every single christian who is open to God's inspiration as it widens out to a host of souls and becomes a collective whole, a phenomenon of many souls in unison, a phenomenon, in short, of "catholic action." It is the christian people, rising to its feet as if driven by a charismatic grace reawakened out of the dawn of christianity and transforming itself into apostles: ". . . your sons and daughters will be prophets. Your young men shall see visions, and your old men shall dream dreams; and I will pour out my spirit in those days upon my servants and hand-maids, so that they will prophesy" (Acts 2: 17-18).

It is the waves of Pentecost that spring out of the Church's inner depths and enrapture it. And we hear two voices—so very different one from the other, yet each directed towards the same end—express this wave in a sensible form: the one clear, repetitive, insistent, is the voice of the Church's authority calling its eager children to become apostles; the other confused, sorrowful, almost enveloped in a mystery of anguish and hope for the world—for our world is the voice of one imploring without even being conscious of doing so, as a delirious sick person implores someone to come and save him. You might call to mind Paul's vision at Troas: "Here Paul saw a vision in the night; a certain Macedonian stood by him in entreaty, and said, Come over into Macedonia, and help us" (Acts 16: 18).

This vision can be experienced again by anyone who wishes to contemplate both the boundless darkness of our world, deprived of spiritual light, and the voice of mankind aflame with unquenchable thirst for the unknown God whom the apostle invokes as his guide and his salvation. "You are the light of the world" (Mt 5: 14). A great apostolic and missionary calling is passing over our christian generation, almost as if we were charged with a new vocation, and as if our own potential destiny were being revealed to us.

The Sphere of the Apostolate

At last the mission starts to move. Mission means sending. But what is it that the mission carries? Where is it going? What makes it up? These are some of the questions that we must ask, and that in themselves would suffice to occupy us with as many separate problems. And now we are in a position to look at these questions in a comprehensive manner, as we might survey a panorama in perspective.

By now we might even say that we know everything. If the Church is the continuation of Christ, then its mission is to bear him within its folds and to bring him to life in the world, for the Church is our mother. As mother Church it incorporates us into Christ, as St. Paul teaches. In order to describe the Church special terms are needed "most of which are impossible to translate into any other language except by means of either a barbarism or a paraphrase. The Apostle has either invented or brought these terms back into circulation in order to express the ineffable union of christians with Christ in a comprehensible, practical language."[8] It is through the prepositions "with" and "in" that we are born, live, suffer, die and rise from the dead with and in Christ, and it is by means of the Church's ministry and mystery, Christ's mystical body, indeed "Christ's very fullness,"[9] that we accomplish these things.

After all, Christ has spoken; he is the word of God made flesh. Christ is the teacher and the Church will speak, teach and repeat his very words. The Church is a teacher and its mission is to teach, protect, interpret and proclaim God's doctrine. Once again its mission is the school, and its missionaries are catechists, teachers, instructors, professors, preachers, doctors, bishops, the pope.

Again: Christ has lived among us men (cf. Bar 3: 38), and by his own example has shown us a model of how we should live. The imitation of Christ can furnish an outline for a new ethic, a model for renewed human virtues, a way to an ascetic and heroic life. Christ has fulfilled his temporal life by the

8. Ferdinand Prat, S.J., *Theology of St. Paul* (Westminster: Newman Press, 1946), II, p. 20.
9. Cf. *ibid.*, pp. 242-243.

sacrifice of the cross and has redeemed the world by his passion and resurrection. In short, he has acted as a priest and his priesthood has been communicated to the Church which will continue it until the consummation of history. The Church's sacramental life constitutes its vital mission and is the treasure that it holds, constantly regenerates, and distributes as widely as possible.

The sacramental life is the treasure that the Church distributes, but to whom? To its children. And where does it find its children? In the world. Hence it is that the Church encounters the world and engages it in a dialogue. If we reflect carefully for a moment we shall realize that this is the aspect of our theme that has been of the greatest interest to our Congress, namely the object of the Church's mission, the sphere of the apostolate.

The picture that we have been sketching comes to life as we make it our own through experience. Let us even say that it takes on a dramatic form, for the encounter of the Church with the contemporary world is in fact a drama as absorbing and complex as it is mysterious and realistic. It is the true drama of history. Our picture becomes larger in scope as heavenly and earthly powers engage in a transcendental struggle on a human battlefield (cf. Eph 6: 12), until providence resolves it in a final epilogue. Here the apostolate becomes an army. Here it becomes an art, assuming methods and theories, and equips itself with concrete instruments for practical action. Here it is passed on by those who have been invested with full responsibility to those who gradually come to participate in this responsibility. It stretches out in many different forms, from those that are spiritual such as prayer and reparation to those that are auxiliary and unmeasurable as it were, such as good words and good deeds. Here the apostolate is classified according to a scale that measures the different types of efficiency: availability, presence and action; here the object of study is the environment in which the apostolate is to take shape and which is examined according to sex, age, social condition and relative capability for receiving or rejecting the christian message. This is a capability that is classified as hostile, recalcitrant, difficult, docile, open.

Confronting the Contemporary World

Pope Pius XII, you may well remember, addressed you in a magistral audience on October 14, 1951, during the first World Congress of the Lay Apostolate and summed up admirably the Church's mission in this respect: "As to the Church, it offers everyone a three-fold mission to be carried out: to raise the ardent believers to a level high enough to meet the demands of our age; to invite those who tarry on the threshold into the warm and healthy intimacy of the home; and to lead back to religion those who have left, since the Church cannot abandon these people to their wretched lot."[10]

I shall restrict myself to sharpening rather than satisfying your interest in this aspect of our theme, the contact between the Church's mission and the contemporary world, by advancing a few simple observations.

1) This aspect has to do directly with the lay apostolate because, if for no other reason, the layman lives in the very world that it is the Church's mission to penetrate. Laymen do in fact have a greater experience of the world than the clergy, for they are the closest witnesses of the contact between the Church's mission and the world that they experience in their concrete lives. It is precisely here that the layman begins to cooperate with the hierarchy by engaging in a sustained study of the contemporary world and by calling attention to what he discovers. The layman cooperates by keeping the clergy informed. Statistical studies and research in religious sociology, conducted under the watchful eye of an expert clergy, can be very profitable, and have in fact already begun to

10. *A.A.S.*, 1951, 786.

yield results that may be used in pastoral work. Thus all studies of the environment, the vast literature of psychological diagnosis and description of social conditions, the examination of existing laws, the discoveries of modern pedagogy and of advertising and so forth, all this constitutes an excellent contribution that the layman can make to help those who are entrusted with the responsibility of guiding the Church's mission.

2) The problem concerning contacts between the Church's mission and the world is a problem that remains perpetually open. For the world, especially today, is undergoing a radical and very rapid evolution, and the realization and proclamation of the christian message take place in different ages under diverse forms. Yet it is the duty of the Church's government to determine when the time is ripe for a given reform, and which reform is actually to be carried out. This is a canon that must especially be called to the attention of laymen since they are easily dazzled by the immediacy of their experience. Less learned as they are in the general criteria governing the Church's life, they often become impatient through excessive zeal, and would like at times either to introduce arbitrary innovations or to hasten reforms in canon law and Church custom without possessing the necessary authority or synoptic vision, or the Holy Spirit's assistance for introducing them. The very experiments that lay apostles suggest as legitimate and ingenious innovations should always be carried out with the assistance and approval of ecclesiastical authority. Yet this is no negative rule, for it contains the secret of our Catholic strength. Let us recall the words of St. Ignatius of Antioch: "In matters concerning the Church let nobody do anything without the bishop."[11] In any event, let us have trust, for Rome is on the move and the pope is there to guide it along.

3) The distinction between the sacred and the profane

11. St. Ignatius of Antioch, *Ad Smir.*, VIII.

deserves a special and attentive examination, as this problem lends itself to serious and harmful misunderstanding and can easily end up in a mistaken solution. Both extremes are obvious: the absolute separation of the sacred and the profane can completely paralyze or neutralize the Church's mission, and modern secularism knows this very well. It exploits the apparent respect for sacred things in its effort to exclude them from day-to-day existence. It is also known that a confusion of sacred with profane interests and morals involves a violent contradiction both of the transcendent character of religion and of the purity of the christian message. Moreover, the Church's mission certainly consists in bringing the sacred into a clear relationship with the profane so that the sacred may be communicated rather than corrupted while the profane may be sanctified rather than altered. We are now in the presence of the mystery of the incarnation, of God made man, as it continues throughout history. It is a mystery that is easy to assert but extremely difficult to live. In this field the Church's magisterium should be very helpful and decisive for us, and the studies in christian humanism that are being carried out by Catholic philosophers and scholars should make a solid contribution to both our thought and our action. The subject matter is delicate and by its nature both complex and mutable; it must be examined with prudence and competence.

4) There is yet another problem that I shall also leave unresolved but that I believe might be proper for me to mention at this point. I am speaking of what might be called the problem of "representative gradualism." As apostolic action (the layman's, especially) moves from the inner sphere of the Church and its religious finality, and gradually reaches out into the temporal order and its this-world finality, it loses its capacity to represent the Church and to discharge its mission directly. The lay apostle's activity becomes gradually detached from its central point of departure and responsibility; at first religious, it soon becomes Catholic

Action and then may become an action that is social, economic, artistic, political, or private. At a certain point the mission ceases to be specifically ecclesiastical and becomes what is known today as aconfessional. Even this gradualism is to be studied and defined by ecclesiastical authority. And it is well to remember that religious and moral principles are operative in every sphere, even in the temporal, and that in all his activities, no matter how profane, a Catholic must never leave God's law out of account; on the contrary, he must always retain an apostolic spirit and at least enlighten the christian faith by means of a virtuous life.

5) Finally, the most general and primordial aim of the Church's mission is to engender love for what it announces, lives and propagates. A certain tinge of optimism and success touches the apostolic act. The message is indeed called "the Gospel"—that is, the good tidings—and it is with a song of angelic joy on Christmas night that the good news is announced: "I bring you good news of a great rejoicing for the whole people. This day, in the city of David, a Saviour has been born for you, the Lord Christ himself" (Lk 2:11). The christian message is no prophecy of our damnation; on the contrary, it summons us to repent so that we may be saved. The christian message is neither harsh nor peevish, neither rude nor ironic nor pessimistic. On the contrary, it is generous, powerful and joyful; full of beauty and poetry, of vigor and majesty. Yes, it does indeed exalt the cross with its sorrow, sacrifice and death though its purpose is to bring consolation, redemption and life.

The Testimony of Love

For these reasons the first task for the apostle, for laymen especially, is to offer the world a christian experience that is admirable, attractive and agreeable.

We ourselves should be the first witnesses through our own

union and reciprocal love and through our own inner, heart-
felt and social cohesion. Our Teacher is our witness: "Love
one another." And again: ". . . you are to love one another;
[that] your love for one another is to be like the love I have
borne you. The mark by which all men know you for my
disciples will be the love you bear one another" (Jn 13:
34-35). Tertullian wrote the first apologetics for the nascent
christian community: "See, the people say, how greatly they
love one another" (Ap 39).

The second apologetics will urge us to love those whom
we intend to evangelize. Such is the supreme purpose of the
apostolate, moved as it is by a solicitude for the *other* rather
than by any personal interest, whose aim it is to serve rather
than to conquer, and whose rigorous intransigeance to error
is designed to redeem rather than to damn.

And here arises another great practical problem: apostolic
love leads us to approach the world that we are to convert
even though that very act may contain elements dangerous
for our faith. It is St. Paul who authorizes us to became a
Jew to the Jews and a weakling to the weaklings: "I have
made myself everybody's slave, to win more souls" (1 Cor
9: 20ff). How far does this apostolic relativism extend?
How far the intransigeance? And to what extent are Catholics allowed to be tolerant? It is for those who guide the
Church to decide, because the question is extremely delicate.[12] We shall be vigilant for fear lest our loving and respectful attitude towards non-Catholics may degenerate into
an indifference, an eclecticism, an attraction, even a deser-
tion—for this is what happens to those who study the thought
of others, are at home in a secular society, assume the
customs of the world in order the better to reach it, and urge
toleration of dissidents so vigorously that they end by justi-
fying the opinions of those same dissidents. This happens

12. Cf. Vermeersch, *La Tolérance.*

also to those who entertain a dialogue with strangers while offending their neighbors, to those who are ready to exchange the priest's vestments for the worker's overalls, to those finally who speak of an opening so that they may leave the house rather than call back those who have left. Let us be watchful, I say, and never forget that the fundamental attitude of Catholics who wish to convert the world must be a love of the world, for in this lies the genius of the apostolate: to know how to love.

I should like us to adopt this christian precept as our aim and program here in Rome, the center of the Catholic apostolate. We shall love both neighbors and strangers. We shall love our country as well as the country of others. We shall love our friends as well as our enemies. We shall love Catholics, schismatics, Protestants, Anglicans, the indifferent, Moslems, pagans, atheists. We shall love all social classes, and especially those in the greatest need of help, of assistance and advancement. We shall love children and old people, the poor and the sick. We shall love those who mock us, despise us, oppose us and persecute us. We shall love those who deserve to be loved as well as those who do not. We shall love our enemies. In so far as we are men, we wish no one to be our enemy. We shall love our own age, our own civilization, our own technology, our art, our sports— our entire world. We shall love and endeavor to understand, to have compassion, to value, to serve, to suffer. We shall love with Christ's heart: "Come to me, all you that labour and are burdened . . ." (Mt 11: 28). We shall love with God's breadth: "God so loved the world . . ." (Jn 3: 16).

Is it too much to say that we must love the whole world? Are we exaggerating? Are we so overcome by enthusiasm that we have become arrogant and too demanding? What has become of humility? It does not vanish; on the contrary, it persists along with our vision of reality. And as it is the Church's mission to open up these vast horizons, it is neither presumptuous nor foolish of us to lift up our eyes to God's heaven; for this is our hope and our prayer.

In any event, God's kingdom already exists potentially within us. I can already see a magnificent scene spread out before my eyes, and would like you to listen with me to Christ's words: "Why, lift up your eyes, I tell you, and look at the fields, they are white with the promise of harvest already" (Jn 4: 35).

Dearest brothers, sons and friends, as I look I see you gathered here from all the corners of the earth as you journey to Rome along the path of unity, and as you prepare to return to the world along the ways of Catholicism. Do not ask me then to speak to you any longer, as perhaps I should, of those who are entrusted with carrying out the Church's mission, for this is all too well known: it is the apostles who do this. Moreover, today it is likewise known and is in fact true that you laymen, Catholics of all nations, are called to cooperate in bringing about this mission in such a manner that it may become your very own. Yes, the mission must become your own.

The Charity of the Church Towards the Alienated

The Church's Universalistic Program

The Center for Pastoral Orientation has chosen Milan for its annual Week of pastoral "aggiornamento" not because our city claims to teach anything original, but in order to furnish us with a welcome opportunity to define and discuss certain problems at a time when they are becoming, perhaps above all in Milan, both grave and pressing. Moreover, in this Week we are given an opportunity of resuming thoughts and suggestions that the citizens' mission proposed last year. These thoughts and suggestions still require to be followed up in relation to the encouraging experience and wisdom of our fellow men.

We are therefore grateful to those who have organized this Week and to all who have participated in the program. We are also confident that these brief and intense days have engendered a unity of intention and prayer. This, we hope, will help in giving all of us (especially us Milanese, who need these things more than others) a fresh pastoral vigor, a clarity of thought, an eagerness and a grace that will enable us to carry out our apostolate on a larger scale and in a more satisfactory fashion.

The topic that engages us in this Eighth Week of pastoral "aggiornamento" is, as you know, the problem of the "alienated." This is a word that immediately raises a host of problems and calls forth a variety of principles and observations.

The expression means that the Catholic religion plants itself at the center of each human destiny, and from its first appearance virtually determines and defines each one. Jesus Christ, the world's light, rises from the midst of mankind and fixes its pivotal character. He divides the book of history into two and only two great pages, the Old and the New Testament, and bestows a coherent and transcendent meaning on the countless and conflicting vicissitudes of civilization. He affects the fate of the cultures of different peoples, and even more directly and more fatally, the destiny of every single human being. Christ asserts himself as teacher, savior, judge, archetype, and as the head of mankind. And St. Paul is the first apostle of the Gentiles, that is, of the alienated. He is also the first to express the concept of Christ in theological terms. In fact, his entire doctrine may be summed up in the two-fold affirmation of the sufficiency and necessity of our Lord Jesus Christ.

From the time of its birth christianity has asserted that it is universal. In order that it be so in fact as it is by right, one law (that is to say, the apostolate) and one organism (that is to say, the hierarchy) have engaged in an endeavor to approach, instruct, attract and unite all men of all times and all places into one new, vast, sovereign, visible but at the same time supra-temporal religious society, the Church. This program is enormous in range, yet we are no longer free to reject it. It is a program that can never be finished, but it is perpetually sustained by our consciousness that it represents the world's highest destiny. It is an original program and one that takes advantage of the organized structures that have been created, one by one, throughout man's secular

history. It is a program that supports, broadens and helps
these perspectives by stimulating a desire for peace, unity
and universality. Yet it is prepared to surpass those same
structures the moment they display their contingency, and is
equally prepared to damn them if necessary the moment they
find support in such anti-human principles as tyranny,
imperialism, egotistic capitalism, communism and every
kind of false brotherhood. It is a relentless program indeed,
springing as it does from the inescapable responsibility that
is aflame in that part of mankind that is already constituted
in Christ's Church, a responsibility that continues to agitate
and torment it.

The program continues its relentless course as it fills man's
tender heart with superhuman boldness, infuses it with inexhaustible heroic energies, triumphant missionary plans,
powers of unlikely sacrifices and a generous range of hopes
never disillusioned. In short, the universal program that
arises within the Church springs from Christ's redemption
and is charged with the love that is necessary for the Church
to become in fact what it is in name, by constitution and in
its genius: truly Catholic.

The beauty, both majestic and dramatic, of this word
"Catholic" should be a source of admiration and respect for
anyone possessing a sense and a vision of great human
events. It could by itself reveal the ignorance of those secu-
larists among us who do their utmost to ignore and repress
its use in the living language of our society. They attempt
this the very moment so many young people, both studious
and idealistic, go about searching for it in the seductive
manifestations of a threatening materialistic universalism.
The word must not be forgotten and suppressed by those
engaged in spreading the name of Italy throughout the world
by civil means, nor must it be distinguished—let alone separated—from the term "christian" (whence "Catholic" draws
both its justification and substance) by those who insist on

a materialistic and spiritualistic regeneration. But for us fortunate enough to enjoy the responsibility of using it as a sign by which we are baptized and marked as Catholics, this word should always be a living source of religious and human consciousness, forever aflame and forever arousing in us a desire to join our fellow men in a relationship of faith and charity.

The Problem of the "Alienated"

For the Catholic nobody ought to be alienated. This is the problem. And since as a matter of fact the alienated do exist—in ever growing numbers and with an increasingly hostile disposition—our problem promptly reaches colossal proportions.

Let us, in a summary fashion, divide our problem into three parts. The first part mentioned above, and the subject of my short introduction, embraces the Church's love for the alienated: that is, the reasons why the Church must concern itself with them, and its attitude towards carrying out its untiring mission.

The second part includes and describes how the apostolate works: that is, the means, methods and forms whereby the christian message is preached from the moment that some men are entrusted with the task of conveying it to their fellow men. We are speaking of that concrete social ministry which Christ has willed to link to the fate of his Gospel. The Gospel (let us note) is neither a simple, self-propagating doctrine nor a book sufficient unto itself: it is a religion in need of a human channel, a religion that finds fulfillment in an organized and visible society. Consequently countless and diverse problems arise regarding the means, that is, the channels of communication between the source and the alienated.

The third part concerns the alienated themselves as they

are divided up and arranged in an elusive casuistry. This is so variegated and so rich that it embraces a comprehensive examination of entire civilizations and requires us to enter into a profound analysis of the most intimate and evanescent feelings of every human heart.

The Church's Love for the "Alienated"

Let us confine ourselves briefly for the moment to the first part, the *terminus a quo* of this wondrous and mysterious drama. It has to do with man's calling to the Gospel, his salvation, rather than with any endeavor to win him over. In fact, the theme assigned for us to consider together is precisely this: "the Church's charity towards the alienated."

We shall not treat the theme in its doctrinal aspect, but shall be satisfied with a simple reference to the universal character of the redemption and to the institution of the apostolic office of the hierarchy. We could easily discuss a great many aspects of Catholic doctrine related to our theme, such as the revelation of God's mercy, the generosity and discipline of penance, the theoretical foundations of missionary evangelization, the relationship between truth and charity, the teaching of dogma through preaching, and so forth. We shall restrict ourselves to a survey of the actual conditions governing the practice of the Church's charity in providing the alienated with the benefits of its Gospel and its charismatic powers.

Today the practice of this charity, viewed on the grand apostolic scale of the Church, is both highly esteemed and greatly successful. The evangelizing effort of the Church displays admirable results before our very eyes, and we do in fact possess evidence of both the apostolic vitality of the Church's perennial youth and of the Holy Spirit's assistance in guiding and sustaining it. No religion is as conscious of its universality as is the Catholic religion, and in no earlier age has this consciousness released such apostolic energies within the Church as it has in our own age. Indeed, our very age, marked as it is by the decline of all religions and by the upsurge of widespread apostasies and a growing hostility even among nations that once constituted christendom and took pride in their faith—our very age is no less marked by an apostolic revival within the Church itself. It is enough to recall a two-fold phenomenon. One is the missionary event that has been assuming world proportions, even though it is still unequal to the immense fields in which it dares test its strength and even though it is harassed and opposed in a great many regions where it has shown that it is capable of development. The other is the organizational event that involves the Catholic laity, especially in the ranks of Catholic Action, that has offered its cooperation by complementing the work of the hierarchy through supporting the civil and religious mission and through widening the apostolic range.

Let us mention just a few additional and magnificent forms in which apostolic charity works within the Church today, and let us begin with the spreading of Catholic culture in our schools, universities, books, magazines, and theaters by such a variety of means as to qualify it as a science, an apologetics, a doctrine, a literature, a press, an art. Catholic thought is neither asleep nor buried in past codes, nor has it lost its capacity and eagerness to engage our contemporary culture in a dialogue. It is enough for us to recall the monumental collection of pontifical addresses in order to see how the highest office of the teaching Church has been engaging, day after day as it were, in an illuminating dialogue with the various and authoritative representatives of science and modern life.

There is another manifestation that likewise bears witness to the Church's solicitude to help us share in the benefits of its faith and civilization. It is the elaboration of a social doctrine. Both human and receptive, this doctrine acknowl-

edges that the changes which modern life brings about in
social structures are both right and inevitable—and it is imperative that as the new institutions arise they should find,
already formulated, a general plan of justice and human
goodness. At the same time the social doctrine should make
sure that the new institutions will be turned neither against
the working classes nor the very economic and social order
for whose sake they were chiefly instituted.

The Church's "Relativism"

We might also call to mind another phenomenon that is
wider in scope and more complex, but no less significant for
the purposes that prompt mother Church, solicitous in her
charity, to smooth the way to the fold for the alienated. I
am speaking of the Church's "adaptation" to the thought,
customs, "trends" and particularly languages of the men of
our own age, engulfed as they are in the processes of our rapid
and complex civil evolution and exacting as they are in their
preferences and personalities. This is the "relativism" of the
Church that, precisely in virtue of being catholic, every day
reveals new attitudes that allow it to accept, assimilate, purify
and even sanctify the most varied forms of human living.

Here for example is how Pius XII spoke of this phenomenon in reference to one of its most delicate points: ways of
teaching the immutable truths of Catholic doctrine. In addressing the General Congregation of the Society of Jesus
he urged the Society not only "to venerate the truth of faith
above everything else but also to acquire accurate and perfect knowledge. Moreover, in the footsteps of their own
illustrious Institute they should follow the course of the
doctrine as much and as closely as possible, convinced that
by espousing this method, however difficult it might be, they
would be of great help to the glory of God and the edification
of the Church. Moreover, they must address themselves

through speech and writing to the men of their age and make themselves understood clearly and willingly. Whence we may infer that, in raising and treating problems, in adducing relevant arguments as well as in their very method of exposition, they should adapt themselves wisely to the character and spirit of their age."[1]

Thus in the very encyclical *Humani Generis* that checks in a positive way the spread of theories that subvert christian dogma, we also find moderated assertions and exhortations that encourage positive studies, both scriptural and scientific.[2]

We might also mention the open possibilities of innumerable dialogues between dissident christians and Catholics, aimed at facilitating their return to the unity of the Church.[3]

Again, we might mention the incipient use of living languages in the liturgy. We could speak at greater length of official relations between the Holy See and non-Catholic countries; of the frequency with which the last few popes have exhorted all believers in God—of any religion whatsoever—to join forces in resisting the encroachment of atheism; and of the Holy Father's reception in his audiences of people from all corners of the world and from all walks of life.

Do not ask me at this time to show you the results of these and similar acts through which the Church wishes to reach the alienated. That is for another occasion. Right now I am interested in calling your attention to the well documented desire of the Church to make it easy for the world to accept the Gospel. The Church is prompt in removing obstacles and is eager to clear the way; it is ready to engage in dialogue and to maintain a vigilant and maternal spirit in order to dispense as widely as possible the salvation entrusted to it. The Church does not maintain closed and impenetrable

1. *A.A.S.*, 1946, 384.
2. *A.A.S.*, 1950, 575ff.
3. *A.A.S.*, 1948, 257; 1950, 142ff.

positions, nor does it threaten and issue anathemas. It does not clothe itself in a complacent indifference and shut itself off from a world that neither understands nor wants it. On the contrary, the Church's law is apostolic charity.

Yet we must insist on one fundamental point that distinguishes the Catholic Church from all forms of ecumenism that are compromising in matters of faith and oppose the unified hierarchical constitution of the Church. It is impossible for the Church to deny or minimize the truth in order to accommodate itself to various segments of dissident christians, for the truth is an inviolable deposit entrusted to the Church to be safeguarded and propagated. The Church can not betray the faith, nor can it play upon the equivocal character of a reticence and ambiguity that would radically contradict its mission of fidelity to divine revelation and of witness to the light. It can not remain satisfied with approximative formulations and an indifferent kind of eclecticism without thereby betraying Christ and denying its own identity. Again, the Church must perforce denounce those errors, both within and without its orbit, that turn men's minds away from the right path of religious truth. And let us note that it is precisely this truth, carried into human thought and life, that succeeds in illuminating propositions in philosophy that are indisputable, and in establishing rules that are irrefutable for an exact conception of human life.

We modern men do not find it easy to appreciate the Church's doctrinal stability because we are accustomed to babel-like differences in the philosophical world and the tolerant contradictions of social life. But we must remember that the Church's doctrine is its very reason for existing, while for the world towards which its mission is directed it is the principle of salvation. Truth is salvation and goodness, being and life. Truth is God, and therefore the Church's gift to the world. Truth is the Church's charity in its highest and most indispensable form.

The Necessity of the Pastoral Art

In asserting any one of its truths, therefore, the Church performs an act of charity, and should any man reject the Church in the light of that affirmation, it can neither remain silent nor soften or distort the truth. *Est, est; non, non.* The Church prefers to die and teach with blood what it has been unable to teach through words. In such a case to suffer opposition, hatred, separation, persecution and martyrdom would be an act of mercy. This is the drama and often the tragedy of the Word that has entered into the world: "His own have not received him." First orthodoxy creates the alienated and then seems to block their entry to Christ's fold.

Yet the paths of the pastoral art wind about and stretch out from the sheepfold that is Christ's doctrine. The good shepherd is not content to remain within the sheepfold; the moment he notices that one of his flock is missing he immediately sets out in search of it. Orthodoxy does not satisfy him unless he can share it with everybody. By the nature of things orthodoxy separates and reproaches those who fail to accept it, yet in no way does it authorize us to abandon those who have abandoned it. Orthodoxy does not condone inertia on our part, nor does it engender a spirit of self-sufficiency and pride. It does not remove our sorrow for the separation; it does not lessen anxiety about the outcome of our search. The boundaries of orthodoxy are not those of pastoral charity.

Let us now turn our attention to the apostolic plane and concentrate into one single word the aim of the Church's pastoral charity towards the alienated: approach. This simple word embraces many pastoral meanings. The most general and fundamental is the pastor's initiative towards the alienated, his desire and prayer at least, his hope and heart-felt suffering when he is unable to do anything else.

All this rests first on an awareness, an initial spiritual disposition: a glance beyond the confines of our sheepfold. There is a widespread belief among us that Italy is a Catholic country because, fortunately, the great majority of our people still receives baptism. Yet we are not sufficiently aware of the fact that there are a great many who fail to live in accordance with the dignity and moral obligation which baptism entails. Many pastors, especially in cities, become resigned to restricting their ministry to those who attend church, and often enough this ministry does satisfy and appease their pastoral zeal. But what of the others? And how many are there? We still need a solid, accurate and standardized system of religious statistics, for our studies in religious and pastoral sociology are still in their infancy. Yet we must realize that a very great many of the faithful do not really believe, that the number of those who are alienated exceeds the number of those who have remained, and that in many places the pastoral reach is becoming more restricted.

Pastoral Sensitivity

Our vision is continuously enlarged by charity. It is through charity that we keep a record of the empty places in the paternal home, that we think of the children who do not belong to us as well as of the children who do not belong to us yet. Such is the anxiety that characterizes the good pastor as he thinks about, discovers, recognizes, counts, and longs to know those who are alienated. And so is generated within the pastor a special disposition towards these alienated.

While these people are usually treated as alien, the pastor treats them as still his own. They are, to be sure, strangers and enemies, at times even fierce and astute enemies, but it is they and not the pastor who are responsible for their situation. The pastor will endeavor to maintain his dignity and remain clearly consistent in his ideas and way of life. He will nourish an inner sense of freedom and strength and use a language that is clear and sincere, and at times firm though heart-broken (moral weakness has never served Christ's cause nor has it ever really converted those who are alienated). The pastor will take pains never to offend any person, never to fail in that sense of respect which we owe to every single person and which we christians especially recognize as due to the human person as a free agent. As pastors, again, we should respect those whom we must always consider as men who may possibly return to the paternal home, as possible children and friends tomorrow. This may well be a vain hope, an unwarranted and naive goodness. We must be on guard lest it turn into weakness and connivance, and become deplorable insensitivity. We must also watch lest this same goodness be ensnared by fraud and ridicule, twin adversaries that are capable of every dismal trickery.

All the attitudes that we have mentioned do indeed constitute, collectively, an indispensable condition that enables us to pray, hope and speak. When sufficiently grave reasons fail to justify a polemic that is already prolonged and full of resentment, acid and sarcastic, and when that same polemic is aimed at those who are alienated and remain so, and when it is we the clergy who support it, then it can no longer be counted as one of our pastoral instruments.

Therefore I must deem both inadvisable and self-defeating any preaching that is biting and aggressive, especially if repeated again and again and unsupported by arguments designed to convince rather than wound. Oh, how intensely must we study the art of preaching as it affects the alienated! As we address ourselves to them we must display an unmistakable kindness, firm yet fatherly, sincere yet sorrowful. And we must be ready to reproach when and if necessary, accuse and cry out (the Gospel's "Woe!" more than once issued from Christ's lips). We must be ready to weep, exhort, invite.

In this connection we can see the emergence of one of the most vital and delicate aspects of our problem: the exercise of authority, and especially the manner in which it is exercised. This problem does in fact seem to dominate and disturb the people of our age. When authority is exercised in a manner that is dignified and gentle, refined and solicitous, it attracts people; but when on the contrary it assumes forms that are exacting and inquisitorial, peremptory and rude, it invariably repels. Unfortunately, this failure to be courteous and temperate is one of the most persistent and pernicious causes for the separation of the faithful from their pastor, as well as a sign of great insensitivity to the exigencies of modern education. For today we can no longer tolerate abuse of authority, any kind of ill treatment, or failure to show respect and display good manners. Finally, it would be a mark of serious failure on our part if we should forget that the Church's authority is fatherly, and that it is both service and love.

Not Criticism but Love

Let us attend to another interesting aspect of our problem, still related to our theme of respect for the alienated. There are some who tend to expose and denounce, with penetrating criticism and often bitter irony, all sorts of defects in their neighbors, in their fellow believers, in Catholics. Indeed, these men censure and mock Catholics ever the more relentlessly the more readily their questionable devotion and faulty zeal causes them to be conspicuous. At the same time and with open sympathy these same men call attention to many virtuous and praiseworthy traits in the alienated. While merit and ability are recognized in the alienated, reproach is reserved for our neighbors. Actually this dislocated moral judgment that discovers evil in so-called good people and good in so-called evil people has its origin in the Gospel, for there the Pharisees are treated as worse than publicans and prostitutes.

The dislocated moral judgment does therefore express a christian criterion for renewing virtue. It is a criterion that we must embrace in all humility and sincerity. Our virtue must have sincerity, interiority and humility. It must not dissolve into conventional forms void both of profound human meaning and of divine grace. And we must never lose our respect for and confidence in every human being, because every human being is always capable of an inward regeneration and of a deeper compassion. We must remember, however, that this evangelical process presupposes a divine authority. Even when it becomes inescapable because it is grounded in a solid moral analysis, it must not become a way of life for us. It does not authorize us to insult our brothers so that we may exalt our enemies. We must not alter the moral judgment that we intended to reinstate in the first place. We must not prematurely condemn good-hearted people in order to allow those who deserve censure to continue with their poor ways of thinking and living.

Furthermore, we should see whether those Catholics who have been censured are in fact Pharisees and whether those who have been favored with such indulgence do in fact harbor those feelings of repentance that we find in the sinners whom the Gospel redeems. What we now face is a vice that is rather widespread and has been vastly popular in contemporary literature (see Dostoievski and Mauriac). It is a vice that has made a reputation for distinguished and revered preachers just as it has had followers whose aim seems to be to move away from their neighbors in order to approach those far off.

The moral austerity of these critics deserves respect, though I must be allowed to doubt the value of their method the moment it becomes an habitual manner lacking in humility and charity, capable of engendering and spreading

about a disturbing and hardly unifying spirit and of presenting christianity in a bitter and unilateral fashion. Should this
method become worse it will succeed in quenching any sense
of brotherhood and in substituting for it hybrid and dangerous friendships. Those who find it intolerable to live in
their father's house will soon find themselves unable to call
back the alienated. At the same time they will find themselves exposed to the danger that not they but the alienated
may well draw their impatient brothers to themselves.

Pastoral Action

What then must pastoral charity do? It is not enough that
it should change and shape the pastor's soul, nor that it
should remain at the level of a pure mental state or of a
simple inner feeling: it must go forth and become active.
I shall limit myself to an examination of the pastor's state
of mind as it becomes transformed into action.

We have said, and let us repeat, that those who elect to
become pastors, that is, seekers of alienated souls, must never
forget let alone undermine and disown the precious and vital
heritage of truth that they bear and must communicate to
the alienated. Furthermore, it is not only truth that the
pastor must preserve intact, but his moral beliefs as well.
There is no doubt about this. Let us take an additional step
and assert that the pastor should not even alter the sincere
and austere mark of his distinctive ecclesiastical presence.
In order to reach another person we must, to be sure, become
like him, "rejoice with those who rejoice; mourn with the
mourner" (Rom 12: 15), but this need not damage the
genuine spirit and even the appearance of Christ's minister.
Those who camouflage themselves by taking on the secular
and worldly forms of the environment in which they intend
to carry out their ministry weaken their own moral strength.
They expose themselves to the danger of accepting the

opinions and beliefs of the other person rather than advancing their own, and arouse the suspicion at times that they themselves are men of little virtue and questionable sincerity. The drama of the worker-priests became aggravated by the priest's excessive desire to assimilate the secular environment, which he first entered with great apostolic zeal only to find himself imprisoned by it, both in body and frequently in spirit.

This is the usual story of the priest who gives in with a complacent and smug unconcern to the adulation and comforts of the refined and upper-class world into which he is called to do some little good. He quickly becomes so enslaved to the environment itself as to lose both the independence and efficacy of his spiritual action. Yet this casuistry is difficult to define, for it frequently affects discipline rather than principles and, more often than not, affects practical conduct alone. It is not doctrine that is at issue here; it is rather a question concerning an art worked out by the pastor under the guidance of his apostolic instinct.

If the pastor does indeed follow and develop a doctrine, it is one that deals with human psychology rather than theology. He sets forth along the pathways of the world, yet has no desire to remain within the world. His purpose is rather to travel the road that will lead him back to the Father along with those whom he has met on the way. Undoubtedly, the road is full of dangers. But we must not therefore make the pastor inaccessible and harsh towards his fellow men, for they are testing such unexplored paths as education, the press, movie criticism, the arts, sports, welfare assistance to workers, the armed forces, emigrants, prisoners, and the rest. We must not make the pastor insensitive and harsh when his superior has authorized him to do these things and he himself is guided by both prudence and charity.

Too often in the past perhaps we have raised a scandal whenever a bold pastor has attempted a fresh and courageous sortie. Risk is part and parcel of the pastoral art. If we do not wish this art to be paralyzed at its very birth we must accept the well intentioned pastoral experiments with a certain largeness of view, and assist and direct them until they have shown sufficient evidence of either their validity or failure. What matters is that we priests should educate our spirit towards a love for the alienated. This is not easy to do, especially in an age such as ours with its radical and disloyal hostility against religion and the Church. It is not an easy task when each one of our good deeds is immediately interpreted as a symptom of either weakness or perfect complicity. Nor again is it easy to do when we have already given ample evidence of a large and humane generosity towards every kind of alienated person, especially in the terrible years of the last war.

It is not easy to do when so many attempts at rapprochement have failed to yield a proportionate and positive result, such as the crusade for the great return of those who have fallen away, or the wide concessions granted to the spirit of freedom, tolerance and democracy. And it is not easy to do when we are faced with dangerous formulas for an opening that may turn out to be of greater benefit to the other person's errors than to our own principles. Nor is it easy to do when yesterday's tyrants go about exploiting today's licence in order to obstruct civil coexistence capriciously.

We must do all this nonetheless, but without reviving the old anticlerical polemic in Italy as if this were an indispensable element in the dialectic of history. The simple reason for this is that we Catholics have already settled the inevitable Roman Question, hold no animosity whatsoever against our country, and conceal no aspirations either temporalistic or theocratic in nature. On the contrary, we wish to serve our country, our institutions and our fellow citizens with the utmost loyalty. And we must not allow the slanderous belief to take root that simply because it has been the Church's duty to condemn atheistic communism it has thereby become an enemy of the working classes, and has come to support juridical and social regimes that oppose their interests. On the contrary, with consistent vigor and coherent performance we must realize in the concrete the christian social doctrine and the pope's oft repeated guiding norms. On this vital point it is imperative that the Church which has already proven its undaunted and unyielding firmness in defending truth should give an even greater proof of its inexhaustible and indefatigable charity: "We are to follow the truth, in a spirit of charity," St. Paul teaches (Eph 4: 15). Let us then join our pastoral charity to our defence of doctrine.

We must do both, I insist. Perhaps the chief result of this Week's work will be the opening of our souls as priests and pastors to a love for the alienated, a result that will be free of great programmatic deliberations and practical achievements. But the result will not be meager if, once again, we should become more faithful disciples of the Master who has come not "to call the just; but sinners to repentance" (Lk 5: 32), who has admonished us that "it is those who are sick, not those who are in health, that have need of the physician" (Lk 5: 31), and that if we love those alone who love us, we deserve no merit whatsoever (cf. Lk 6: 33). Let us remember that he reproached the Apostles for becoming angry when the Samaritans denied hospitality to their weary Master, a pilgrim, and for being so eager to call down the fire of heaven upon those country people: "You do not understand what spirit it is you share" (Lk 9: 55).

Let us also remember that to the Apostle Peter's question: "How often must I see my brother do me wrong, and still forgive him; as much as seven times?" he replied: "I tell thee to forgive, not seven wrongs, but seventy times seven" (Mt 18: 22). We shall then appreciate and find it profitable to remember that our Lord "has allowed us to minister this reconciliation of his to others" (2 Cor 5: 18-19), and that it is precisely the priest's mission to be called to such an office so that he may "experience compassion for" (*condolere*) —have pity on and share in—the lot of the unfortunate: "being able to feel for them when they are ignorant and make mistakes, since he, too, is all beset with humiliations" (Heb 5: 2).

Now then, most venerable brothers, we have reaped a good harvest, for we have reached a better understanding of our mission and have learned to translate our devotion to the sacred heart of Christ into a great pastoral force. Finally, we have learned to put before everything else two means for securing the welfare of the alienated, two means that are rooted in the Church's charity and in our own spirit: a genuine presentation of Christ's religion; and our own prudent, diligent, zealous and patient personal approach.

The Secret of the Cathedral

Let Us Salute the Church of Crema!

L et us salute it in its renovated cathedral, in its worthy pastor, the bishop who has succeeded in accomplishing this delicate and life-giving restoration. Let us salute it in its clergy whom we see gathered here and whom we know to be zealous and of one mind; in its people, industrious and honest, who are faithful to its religious and civil traditions and find here the most distinguished monument of its history as well as an affirmation of its faith and culture. Let us salute it in the name of those who have come here to honor it today, the bishops of Lombardy, the civil authorities of Cremona and Crema, and in the name of those who have dedicated their labor to the artistic renewal of this cathedral. And let us salute it in the name of the Ambrosian city that takes pride in the recaptured beauty and spiritual warmth of this, a sister cathedral.

Let us salute it in the name of Mary most holy, who here too is especially venerated, in the name of the angels who stand watch over this church, and of the saints to whom it is dedicated and whose holy relics it preserves. Let us salute it in memory of those christian generations that have suc-

69

ceeded one another in this place for centuries, and in this
place have prayed and bestowed a religious sense upon life
on earth, and have entertained a hope for a life beyond this
earth.

To salute means to wish for grace, for joy, peace, charity,
the gifts of the Holy Spirit, as St. Paul did.

The Charm of the Cathedral

It seems to me that this exchange of spiritual wishes immediately engenders in us the most suitable state of mind for
entering into this sacred edifice, for contemplating its
austere and majestic lines, for breathing its mysterious air.
A harmony of souls is suitable to these silent spaces and a
gentleness in feeling to the dignity of this mighty structure.
This is exactly what we need; that is to say, we need to attune
our souls to the physical place in which we live, and engage
these very walls in a dialogue as it were.

No other building casts such a penetrating and moving
spell, so that we feel pressed to advance some kind of explanation. It is impossible not to notice this, for even the
tourist looks on attentively and would like to understand the
secret of this structure by means of a few easily dispatched
and magical words of explanation. But those who have no
desire to rush tarry with pleasure, and reflect.

But what makes a cathedral so attractive? What makes
this cathedral so suggestive? Is it the novelty of the work?
Undoubtedly. Yet what enchants us more than the novelty
is the antiquity of the cathedral as it is reconstructed in its
original frame. Is it perhaps the vastness of its dimensions?
Certainly! For us modern men who spend our lives in the
narrow boxes of economy apartments, these sumptuous and
solemn heights enlarge our hearts. There are many other
buildings both high and spacious, yet they fail to speak to
our souls as does this one. Is it perhaps the antiquity that

seems to defy the passage of time, and transport us into a world gone by, crowded with romantic dreams? Yes again, for even this voice seems to echo remote centuries and to emerge from hidden depths like the song of departed souls; it is a voice that causes our emotions to tremble, to tremble as it were with reverential fear. But we notice immediately that we have been dealing with something that is physical and unmovable, and that there is something else that continues to torment us.

Perhaps it is the history etched so splendidly on these stones that, for those capable of deciphering it, has hundreds of tales to tell: marvellous tales of the Middle Ages, full of saints and warriors, with powerful lords and industrious commoners, with the most tender devotions and bloody cruelties.

History does indeed have highly absorbing tales to disclose. It lays bare before us admirable, positive facts that frequently provoke us to think and reconstruct history in fanciful ways and in such a manner as to create the welcome impression that we have at long last captured the meaning of this great mass that, like a surviving ship, floats along on the stormy waters of the centuries.

But we soon find ourselves very quickly dissatisfied even with respect to history, for what we find in this place is no mere document of past historical events. There is something quite different, and eternal. There is not simply a message about past events, but a perpetual song, a manifestation of life. Here we find beauty. Here we find art, an art that intoxicates. In this place we also see an unmistakable manifestation of those two characteristics that, in the opinion of Viollet-le-Duc, the great restorer of French medieval monuments, shape the beauty and power and grace of all structures. In this place too we find, at one and the same time revealed and concealed, a wealth of elements that are distinctive characteristics of that Romanesque-Lombard style which illuminates one of the most beautiful periods in our medieval Christian-Latin culture.

Today we all know that a vast literature, involving great research, has explored the medieval cathedral and indeed brought it to life, even for us who are the late descendants of a vanished age. Yet we retain a capacity to admire and catch a lingering meaning of that world which has been recorded through monuments of such vast proportion and unspeakable beauty.

And here we should like to pause and differentiate between what is distinctive of a given historical and artistic period and what is capable of being treasured by any age, even our own. A cathedral is a building that is thoroughly expressive and pregnant with meanings that stretch beyond what we have mentioned above with respect to antiquity, history and art. For we must realize that one meaning is undoubtedly paramount, and that is the religious meaning—though even this vital aspect of the cathedral, the religious aspect, is revealed to us in a special way. There is no doubt that a cathedral differs from a catacomb, a sanctuary and a monastery, though each of these places does possess great religious value. But let us not continue along these lines, for an analysis of this problem would carry us away.

The Cathedral Is an Expression of Unity

Let us pause to consider only two characteristics of this religious meaning, the one an expression of hierarchical order, the other of unity. We all know that a cathedral rests on a summit and is like the "city on the mountain" of which the Gospel speaks. Its very mass stands witness to this sublime fact in a testimony that is not only external and architectonic but spiritual as well, for it announces openly the place that is due to religion. The bishop of this cathedral has expressed this idea well: it "reminds and admonishes men of the primacy of the spiritual." It is the court of God's kingdom, that kingdom that we must seek above everything else. A medieval conception, some will say. An eternal conception, we shall answer, a conception that is true in so far as it interprets our actual position in this concrete world. We are related to God as creatures; and it is the supreme task of religion to invest life with its true meaning and responsibility, its salvation and destiny.

The cathedral is a solemn proclamation of the one and only conception of life that we may profess, and that is the theocentric conception. Through the Middle Ages and the cathedrals that have been handed down to us, we therefore inherit a patrimony that, far from being useless for our age, constitutes an eternal wisdom which our age would be ill advised to reject.

As we reflect on the medieval hierarchy of ideas and values, the cathedral reminds us of a fresh spiritual trait, that sublime genius for unity in which, amidst a host of contradictions, the Middle Ages excelled. It is precisely this unity that we modern men desperately need, and it is for this unity that we yearn, torn though we continue to be by interminable conflicts.

Here the cathedral displays, at one and the same time, that unity of thought and religion through which medieval christianity shaped its character and developed its distinctive consciousness. This is no heritage to be despised. For us Catholics it is still active and triumphant, for it places the Catholic Church among the most singular and exemplary events in the modern world, and certainly in the world towards which our civilization is moving with such anxiety.

The world tends towards unity in so many of its own temporal fields while the Church, which already possesses a unity of its own, goes about offering this unity to others as a stimulus, as an example, as an aid. The cathedral is a spiritual and social expression of the unity of believers, a beacon that shines forth through the age in which we are living, a modern structure, or better still, a foundation that is as it were undisturbed by the flow of time.

As you see, our thought is becoming theoretical and is carrying us away. But the cathedral is right here, and summons us to fresh and more concrete observations and thought, for it has yet to disclose its inmost secret.

I remember the bleak experience I had in visiting certain cathedrals that were born in the Catholic faith, and remained in that faith for centuries, forming a kind of mystical hearth for the devotion and worship of apostles and fathers, of saints and the christian populace. Later, as these cathedrals were taken over by Protestants, their altars were removed, and I saw as it were a huge decapitated body: the hall was still capable of responding to hymn and prayer, yet something vital seemed to be missing, something like a burnt out fire. And I remember another impression, more tender yet no less sorrowful, which I experienced in England this time. I entered magnificent cathedrals and frequently found them empty: for long periods of time empty of the faithful and invariably empty of the heart that for us dwells in the tabernacle—empty, that is, of Christ's mystical and real body. At evening time however the cathedrals became filled with the sweetest of songs, but whence they came I do not know. The whole cathedral seemed to be filled with its own singing, as a single violin producing sweet melodies that at times are as mournful as plaintive wails arising out of statues and tombs, and at other times as serene and brilliant as voices of invisible angels soaring about under those immense Gothic vaults.

The Secret of the Cathedral Is Christ's Presence

In this place to we hear sacred voices. But where can we find the host of this magnificent house? For the cathedral

belongs to Christ. And here I should also echo the words of
Ambrose when he was engaged, at the risk of his own life,
in defending his Church against the heretic Ausentius, who
yearned to conquer it. And I should also record the argument that Ambrose advanced as he stood up to the Emperor:
"Shall we hand over Christ's heritage [to a heretic]? . . . far
be it from me to hand over Christ's heritage."[1]

Every cathedral belongs to Christ. This very church is
his. For him a chair has been established here, and from this
chair his apostles will speak in his place; for him a throne
has been raised and on this throne will sit those who take his
place; for him an altar has been erected and those who enter
into a new life with him will offer up to the Father his very
own sacrifice; for him the "ecclesia," the people with its
bishop, have gathered here and it is to him that they raise
both a hymn of joy and a prayer of sorrow; and from him,
finally, this temple receives its mystery and its majesty.

He is here!

Listen to his voice: "Where two or three are gathered
together in my name, I am there in the midst of them" (Mt
18: 20). And listen to the voice of John the Evangelist, in
the Apocalypse: ". . . Grace and peace be yours, from . . .
Jesus Christ, the faithful witness, first-born of the risen dead,
who rules over all earthly kings. He has proved his love for
us, by washing us clean from our sins in his own blood, and
made us a royal race of priests, to serve God, his Father;
glory and power be his through endless ages" (Ap 1: 4-6).
As he took leave of his apostles he said: "And behold I
am with you all through the days that are coming, until the
consummation of the world" (Mt 28: 20).

And here is how he appeared to John and how we can
envision his presence: "I saw . . . in the midst of these seven

1. St. Ambrose, *Sermo contra Auxentium de basilicis tradendis*, 17-
18: *nos trademus Christi hereditatem? . . . absit a me ut tradam
Christi hereditatem!*

golden candlesticks one who seemed like a son of man, clothed in a long garment, with a golden girdle about his breast. The hair on his head was like wool snow-white, and his eyes like flaming fire, his feet like orichalc melted in the crucible, and his voice like the sound of water in deep flood . . . and his face was like the sun when it shines at its full strength . . . and he, laying his right hand on me, spoke thus: Do not be afraid: I am before all, I am at the end of all, and I live. I, who underwent death, am alive, as thou seest, to endless ages" (Ap 1: 13-18).

He is here!

This is the secret of the cathedral. For the cathedral is neither a mere fascinating architectural monument nor a venerable historical building nor a vast museum of fine arts. Neither is it a solemn lecture hall nor an esoteric music hall reserved for precious ears. For us the cathedral is a living home, a place enriched with God's presence. Hence we may say, in reference to Christ: "He came to dwell among us" (Jn 1: 14). The cathedral is the palace of Christ the king, the schoolroom of Christ the teacher, and the temple of Christ the priest.

Wherever there is a tabernacle, we know that there his real, sacramental presence brings us to our knees in adoration, invites us to contemplate and admits us to communion. But here in the cathedral, in the presence of the most Holy Eucharist, we discover three additional and different manifestations of his presence.

He is present in this place by his authority and he is present as the way; and it is from this place that he guides his Church along the road to salvation. It is here that he is pastor and here in the cathedral that the mission entrusted to the Apostles, "Feed my lambs" (Jn 21: 15) is extended and continued. For here the bishop, pastor of the diocese, is invested with a prerogative, the faculty of jurisdiction, that is still operative in history as an active presence within Christ's mystical body.

Here he is teacher, and hence he is present as truth. Here he holds a chair; here his voice acquires an authentic ring and finds a faithful echo. "He who listens to you, listens to me" (Lk 10: 16). And the bishop, we also know, is the Apostles' successor. Here he is judge (Lk 22: 30) and here his voice resounds sweetly and loudly "as any two-edged sword" (Heb 4: 12).

And again: here he is present in the fullness of his priesthood, that is, of his perfect office as mediator between God and man, and here he is present in the fullness of the sanctifying power that he has also conferred on the Apostles with the highest degree of efficacy. He is now present as life.

And it is here that the bishop, heir to another divine power, the faculty of sacred orders, sanctifies cleric and layman alike; and it is here that he breathes life into Christ's mystical body.

"Whoever has seen me, has seen the Father," Jesus explained to his Apostles at the last supper (Jn 14: 9). Let us now comment on this passage: he who sees the bishop, also sees Christ. And mark well: we wish to make of the bishop neither a privileged hermit nor a prophet endowed with singular charismatic powers nor a saint inimitable in his virtue. The bishop is a thoroughly social man; his whole function is social, for it is projected onto the people and would indeed make no sense were it exclusively personal in nature. The bishop's office acquires its true meaning the moment it becomes a service: "no difference is to be made, among you, between the greatest and the youngest of you all" (Lk 22: 26), Jesus teaches. And let us note that Christ's mystical presence in the operative principle of his Church needs a community of believers, the pastor needs a flock, the teacher needs students and the husband a wife; the Church teaching needs the Church taught so that the true Church may be formed, the Church that Christ loved and for which he "gave himself up on its behalf . . . he would summon it into his own presence, the Church in all its beauty, no stain, no wrinkle, no such disfigurement; it was to be holy, it was to be spotless" (Eph 5: 25ff).

Thus the secret of the Cathedral is Christ's presence in his mystical body. Here indeed is the mystery of the Church, one, holy, Catholic and apostolic!

We Must "Raise from the Dead" the Spirit of the Church

Let us remember, my brethren, that language does not simply reveal meaning but also makes demands on us. And if we are gathered in this place to celebrate the Church's mystery, that means that the restoration of the physical temple will remain incomplete unless it is followed by a restoration of the spiritual temple. As our bishop has well stated, the restoration will remain incomplete unless we "rejuvenate" the people's Church, the Church of souls, the living Church, before we restore the church-temple.

And so the work of restoration must continue. We must restore the society of believers called the Church and bring it back to the original constitutional plan that the cathedral displays. We must arouse in ourselves an authentic "spirit of the Church." And this spirit must arise from the Church's fundamental thought rather than from any one of its occasional and peculiar manifestations. It must arise from the plan that Christ has foreordained, that canon law has shaped and as it were constructed, and that the pope together with the bishops has fulfilled. The plan is so vast in range that all of us can find an honorable and useful place in it. It is, furthermore, a unifying plan that demands sacrifice of us, though what we are asked to sacrifice are the parochialism, the rivalries, the dissensions and the residual manifestations of egotism—all too residual at times!—that enter even into the kingdom of charity that is God's Church.

We must give back to the Church the importance it ought to have in our spiritual life, in our religious vision, in our living Catholicism. And in a spirit of mutual respect, of peaceful coexistence and of harmonious cooperation we must hope to settle the perennial problem of the Church's relations with the state by a joint acknowledgment of the respective sovereignties of the two societies.

Above all, we must breathe a supernatural spirit into the human Church and spiritual life into the physical Church, in the form known today as liturgical life. The bishop of this reborn cathedral had an excellent idea when he decided to celebrate this solemn occasion by a week of study and actual experience in the sacred liturgy. For the liturgy is the cathedral's own voice, the Church's prayer, action and mystery, set in its true place, in its most glorious and mysterious epiphany. It is the liturgy that makes the stones themselves speak; it is the liturgy that matches every dead stone with a living soul; it is the liturgy that discloses and fulfills the secret of the cathedral.

All this it does as, in its full splendor, it brings to life the mystery of Christ's presence, the mystery of Christ the bread of life, priest and victim, of Christ the way, the truth and the life for us, of Christ the Emmanuel who fulfills his promise to journey with us throughout history till the end of time. It is the cathedral with its liturgical worship that brings Christ to life, and it is Christ whom we remember as he has come into the world, whom we praise as he is present and whom we await in the time to come. And as we remember, praise and await together, bound into an intimate union and organized in his mystical body, we find ourselves suspended from him as it were, and yearning for him: "Be it so, then; come, Lord Jesus" (Ap 22: 20).

The Papacy and Unity in the Church

The Concept of the Church's Unicity

We bring this course of Christian Studies to a close on a simple and familiar note since those who have attended have been fortunate enough to listen to and reflect on some splendid lectures, all of which have been relevant to the concluding theme assigned to me. And how indeed can a study of ecclesiastical unity fail to be related, in every one of its aspects, to the center that represents and fosters this unity? For such indeed is the Papacy to which we now turn our attention as to the summit of a solid ecclesiastical pyramid.

There are two additional and sound reasons that exempt us from talking on at length about this topic. The first is the immense range of the topic itself, from whatever angle it be approached, biblical, historical, theological or juridical. In an address such as this we certainly cannot pretend to exhaust the theme, nor even to advance a summary idea of its ramifications. We must content ourselves with a few obvious remarks on the central theme of the Course, the relationship between the Church and the Papacy.

The second reason is grounded in the fact that all of us

81

gathered here are imbued, in different ways and in different degrees, with the doctrine of the Roman Pontificate. In fact for those of us who are Catholics, for those of us who are Italian and, we may add, for those of us who are men of their own age, this theme comes up time and again.

Yet this conclusion, simple as it is, is important, for it is capable of exerting considerable influence on certain tendencies of our life, both spiritual and practical. It is a conclusion that rests on a first affirmation already familiar to all of us who have attended these lectures: unity is the essential and most distinctive mark of Christ's Church, and it is vital for the christian religion. A second and decisive affirmation is this: the Papacy is essential for the achievement of unity in the Church and, in a certain different sense, in the world. In order to reach our conclusions more readily, we must articulate the concept of unity in two different though complementary aspects. We must deal at the outset with the concept of *unicity* that comes into play the moment we assert that the Church is one: that is, one and only one in respect to the hypothesis or claim that a multiplicity of churches is possible.

This is the external aspect of the Church's unity, the aspect that interests both apologetics and fundamental theology, the aspect that brings the Catholic Church into confrontation with those segments of separated christians who claim for themselves the name of the Church that is in itself incommunicable precisely in so far as the Church is one, that is, one and only one.

This is, in my opinion, the aspect that was chiefly considered in the preceding lectures: inescapably, the true Church can only be one. In fact the christian religion disallows multiplicity in subjective doctrine and interpretation. Neither can the Church be embodied in institutions that are separate one from the other, nor is it capable of embodiment in a variety of constitutional structures. Again, the Church can not allow any person to reach God or, more exactly, attempt to reach God through his own formulas and in his own fashion. The Church and the Church alone possesses the secret of the true relationship to God as it has been established by Jesus Christ. Indeed, it is in so far as it bears Christ that the Church is this very relationship that is both a certain and an exclusive means for attaining our salvation.

We are speaking of the aspect revealed in the "mark" of unity that is characteristic of the true Church. Christ has not established a variety of different churches: he has established one and only one. This Church he called his own and it is precisely this Church that can be traced to Peter.

Assuming that Peter did have successors and that they did inherit the keys to God's kingdom (that is, the very same religious powers that Christ bestowed upon Peter), the following conclusion is inescapable: the "mark" of unity or better *unicity* that defines and characterizes Christ's Church —Christ's true, living and perennial Church—is realized in Peter's successor: that is, the Papacy. And it is through its apostolic character that we achieve the unity (that is, the unicity) of the authentic Church.

For us this doctrine is undisputed and quite commonplace though it is discussed, pressed hard and contested in the many controversies among christians. Let us then confirm this doctrine with one beautiful testimony among the very many that evidence its truth. We are speaking of the testimony of St. Cyprian, African bishop and third century martyr, great defender of the Church's unity. He was a precursor as it were in his choice of the criterion of apostolicity as proof of the true Church's unity and authenticity. For it is precisely this criterion that will lead Newman much later from the Anglican to the Catholic Church. In writing and admonishing his people to "watch out for the snares of the devil," St. Cyprian teaches: "As God is one and Christ is one, so is the Church and so is the chair on which our Lord

has established Peter. It is impossible to raise another altar
or create another priesthood, beyond that one altar and that
one priesthood. He who goes about reaping elsewhere is
wasting himself." Strong words follow against anyone who
attempts to challenge this unity.[1]

The Fundamental Idea of Unity

There is yet another aspect to be considered in connection
with the Church's unity and that is its inner consistency, its
intrinsic unity. We are speaking of course more of an inner
trait than of an external mark, and of one that refers to the
mystery of the Church's life. Above all, this unity entails the
destiny of mankind as it is conceived in God's wisdom and
goodness. So conceived, the unity is all embracing, expressed as it is in the cosmic Christ. St. John the Evangelist
and St. Paul the Apostle especially speak to us of these things,
and St. Paul in particular has expressed them in concise and
vigorous language: "Instaurare omnia in Christo" (Eph 1:
10), that is, lead all things back to one head, Christ. Christ
is at the center of the world, at the center of that human
sphere which he has established as a particular society of
believers, which he has nourished with the light of his doctrine and infused with his grace. The Church is a human
society animated by Christ's spirit. The encyclical on the
mystical body explicitly reminds us of this: "Our divine
savior, without intermediaries and by himself, guides and
governs the society he has established, and in fact rules in our
minds and souls. . . . And by this internal guidance he not
only cares for each one of us as 'the pastor and guardian of
our souls' (1 Pt 2: 25), but likewise addresses himself to
the entire Church."[2]

Christ gives the Church unity in faith, unity in grace, unity

1. St. Cyprian, Ep., 43, 5, 2 in Budé, II, p. 107.
2. *A.A.S.*, 1943, 209-210.

in the assistance it receives. The Church is one through this relationship that it enjoys with its one principle, its head and its spouse. It is through the believers' union with Christ that the Church receives its real spiritual and concrete unity. Let us listen again to St. Paul's words to the Ephesians: "You must be eager to preserve that unity the Spirit gives you, whose bond is peace. You are one body, with a single Spirit; each of you, when he was called, was called in the same hope; with the same Lord, the same faith, the same baptism; with the same God, the same Father of all of us, who is above all beings, pervades all things, and lives in all of us" (Eph 4: 3-6).

If we wish to enter into the christian religious sphere we must allow ourselves to be penetrated by this fundamental idea of unity. For it bears the mark of christian genius and the virtue of its inmost consistency and inexorable capacity for expansion, and reveals the mysterious finality of the mercy and beauty of the divine plan for our salvation. Unity is interchangeable with being. Hence God, the being of beings, being in itself, infinite and transcendent, is eminently one. Everything that lives and exists asserts itself as one. As it grows and continues to live it becomes more and more one, and as it draws near to God it aspires towards that union which is an intimation and approximation of unity itself.

Unity is the philosopher's exigency, metaphysical in nature; in its absence any theory of reality and thought would be impossible. Unity is the exigency of the mystics, that is, of those who not only seek to survey and understand the world and life by way of knowledge but also seek for and do in fact achieve a rudimentary yet transforming experience of its stupendous reality.

I venture to insist on this final aspect of our theme because the concept of unity that we must recognize in Christ's Church leads us to the doctrine of the mystical body, an affirmation ever so insistent on the Church's unity and one that is presented in a form that is congenial to the spiritual needs of modern man. It is a form that is congenial because we are led back to its scriptural sources and we can also apply it as a consolation for life as we actually live it.

In fact the encyclical on the mystical body begins in this way: "The doctrine of Christ's mystical body, that is, the Church assembled in the beginning through the Redeemer's own words, focuses in its true light the gift of intimate union with such a sublime head, yet never has this gift been exalted enough. By its excellence and great heights the doctrine of Christ's mystical body invites all those who are moved by God's spirit to meditate upon him and, by illuminating their minds, stimulates them vigorously to perform profitable works in conformity with these teachings."[3]

Hence for us the concept of the one Church must not be purely historical and juridical (that is, related solely to its members, the Church's human and concrete countenance); it must also be understood in relation to Christ and God, as an inner principle of that reality which makes the Church a mystery: that is, God's thought, God's plan, God's work.

Even before it takes historical shape, the Church is one in God's plan that Christ has begun in the Gospel and that he goes about unfolding in time, and resolving in the mysterious kingdom of the after-life. It is one because it is his Church, and it is one because it is the object of its redemptive mission that, according to Christ's supreme prayer, aims at making us all one: *ut unum sint* (Jn 17: 21). The Church is not only the means of our salvation; it is one with, or better will be one with our salvation the moment its sanctifying mission has been completed and it shall be shown that it was the formation of Christ's body (Eph 4: 12-13).

Now this profound unity that originates in the divine idea

3. *A.A.S.*, 1943, 193.

fulfills itself in Christ and tends to its ultimate living and concrete reality in the future life. It expresses itself, indeed,
must express itself in an unequivocal social unity, human and
visible, in which all of us are invited to participate, and to
which we already have the good fortune and the responsibility of belonging.

Our belonging to this unity should be our joy, our pride,
our strength. We should develop a passion for both unity
and unicity within God's holy Church. Through our consciousness of being members of the Church we should learn
a great spiritual lesson from the Old Testament as it recounts
the great love of Jerusalem's citizen for his city, symbol and
pledge of a people burdened with an unhappy history yet
convinced of its special vocation, and sustained by the mirage
of an unquenchable hope.

We citizens of a Jerusalem that is spiritual but for that
reason no less human and historical than the Jerusalem of
Palestine, of a Jerusalem lowered from heaven onto earth in
order to people it with inhabitants to be taken up to heaven,
we citizens should be very enthusiastic about this religious
homeland that is the Church. For in this our mortal life the
Church anticipates our membership in God's eternal city and
inserts us in that web of relations—at first with Christ, then
with God and our brothers—that prepares us for and foreshadows the final unity of the kingdom of heaven.

The Church's Fundamental Composition

It is the Church that inserts us into an intimate community, for the Church is a universal family, a society that
lives in faith and for charity, a system of converging relations that both exalt and redeem human life. Though in
fact one, it is neither a uniform nor a passive oneness that
shapes it into a mere community of brothers; it is rather an
organic and operative oneness that acts as a mother gener-

ating children. The Church, in short, is a composite oneness marvellously compact in its structure.

And here again St. Paul comes to mind, also on the composite oneness of Christ's Mystical Body: "Some he has appointed to be apostles, others to be prophets, others to be evangelists, or pastors, or teachers. They are to . . . build up the frame of Christ's body" (Eph 4: 11-12).

And now it is time to consider the two fundamental components that shape the Church in its living oneness: the one invisible, life-giving and divine we have already described as God's thought, grace and assistance; the other visible element we may now identify as mankind in so far as it believes and is quickened by charity, the "ecclesia sanctorum," the society of christians. We might even speak of a composition of body and soul that makes the Church an entity at one and the same time divine and human, invisible through the gifts that bestow life upon it, visible through the members that compose and continue it through the mystery of the Incarnation.

Next we encounter a composition in the living body of the Church that embraces its organic character and hierarchical structure. It is in virtue of these two marks that the Church presents itself to us in certain respects as a community of brothers, all on the same level of equality, and in other respects as a community of pastors and parishioners in which the former are endowed with specific powers of sanctification, teaching and government that the latter do not possess. The Church is mother; as St. Bede has well stated, "every day the Church generates the Church."[4] St. Ambrose had already asserted: "we are redeemed by the grace that comes solely from the Church."[5]

How does this fact come about whereby an operative prin-

---

4. St. Bede, *Explanatio Apocalypsis*, I, II: *Ecclesia quotidie gignit Ecclesiam.*
5. St. Ambrose, *In Ps.*, 39, 11: *Sola Ecclesiae gratia, qua redimur.*

ciple, a power, is engendered within and for the unity of the Church? How does a community of charity ever become a community of authority? Does the governing organ originate in the community itself, as so many dissidents claim, compelled as they have been by now to acknowledge the necessity for an authority both visible and operative in the ecclesiastical community? Or is it rather the case that authority already exists before the community does, and in fact convenes, creates, sanctifies and directs it? For us the answer is clear, and we are astonished that it is not equally so for all those who acknowledge the authority of the divine word in Holy Scripture.

Let us just recall the celebrated passage in St. John's Gospel in which Christ, after the resurrection, speaks precisely to Peter about the love that binds him to his Father and insists that it is love also that engenders the pastoral act, whose purpose it is to assemble and guide the flock of christians: "If you love me, since you love me—the Lord seems to be saying—feed my flock." In creating a living society of charity the Lord does not make the society itself the cause of the hierarchical power that is to guide it; rather for the sake of that society he himself directly confers authority on those who are to exercise it in his name.

We find a clear commentary on this point in the writings of a theologian who is famous in the history of both the Protestant Reformation and scholastic theology, Thomas de Vio, known as Cajetan (1469-1534). His commentary is relevant, for in evaluating a major and very modern position in Protestant theology, namely that it is the community rather than the Apostles that is heir to the christian message, Cajetan writes:

To understand her regime, you have only to look at her beginnings. She did not emerge from any collectivity or community whatever. She was formed around Jesus Christ her Head, her Ruler, from whom all her life, perfection and power came to her.

"You have not chosen me," he said, "but I have chosen you." Thus from the birth of the Church her constitution clearly appears. Authority does not reside in the community; it never passes, as in the civil order, from the community to one or to several heads. By its very nature, and from the very outset, it resides in a single recognizable prince. Since this prince is the Lord Jesus, who is to live and reign yesterday, today, and for ever, it results that in natural right it was for him and not for the ecclesiastical community to choose for himself a vicar, whose role it would be not to represent the ecclesiastical community, born to obey not to command, but to represent a Prince, the natural Lord of this community. That, then, was what our Lord himself deigned to do when . . . he chose . . . the Apostle Peter alone for his Vicar. And just as in natural right the Prince of the Church does not draw his authority from the Church, so neither does his Vicar, who depends upon him and not upon the Church.[6]

Moreover, the history of the Church unequivocally proves that it is the hierarchy, the apostle, the missionary who evangelize mankind, and obtain believers out of mankind so that they may be shaped into a living Church. It is not the other way around; it is not a shapeless and capricious community of believers that engenders from its inmost recesses the pastor who is then to administer it.

Both this two-fold duality—the invisible life-giving act and the visible community on the one hand, and the Church teaching and the Church taught on the other—and this source of Christ's authority to govern are essential for the genuine unity of Christ's mystical body.

Now, as we search for the highest and fullest manifestation of this ministry of grace, truth and guidance that reflects and generates this mysterious unity in and through Christ both in time and history we are obliged to conclude that we do find such a manifestation in the person, the concrete, living human person who is visible as Peter's successor: namely, the Pope.

It is in the Pope that the Church centers its unity.

6. Cajetan, *Apologia de comparata auctoritate papae et concilii*, c. 1, n. 450-452. Cf. Journet, *op. cit.*, I, p. 422.

The Relations between the Pope and the Church's Unity

It is well for us to remember that the Church's unity involves neither a pure uniformity of doctrine nor a "bibliocracy," as Calvin's city has been called. It does not involve a simple disciplinary obeisance to one sole hypothetical code of beliefs and customs, nor conformity to a community of believers organized in a compact and monolithic association in the sacred name of the Church. It is neither the sum total of different and divided bodies linked by an imprecise ecumenical bond, nor is it simply the product of a religious society governed either by a college of bishops or by a group of patriarchs: that is, by a hierarchy without a head. It is rather the form, that is, the mark and property, the beauty and life, the mystery of all the peoples gathered into a religious and visible society under the joint rule of the bishops and of their head the Pope, bishop of Rome and of the whole world.[7]

This personification of the Church's unity obliges us to make a good many additional observations but we must perforce simplify. And just as those who have arrived at the summit of a mountain feel compelled to contemplate the panorama spread before their eyes, so must we of necessity single out the pathways that lead to the summit. We must, that is, enumerate some of the relations between the Pope and the unity of the Church.

The first relationship to be considered, that between Christ and the Pope, is a relationship of derivation. Christ, sole and supreme head of the Church, now become heavenly and invisible, makes Peter and each succeeding pope his vicar and hence the terrestrial and visible head of the Church, while he remains the head everlastingly one and the same.[8] Christ's word, love and authority become transformed in the

7. Cf. St. Ambrose, *In Lk*, II, 86.
8. Cf. *Mystici Corporis, A.A.S.*, 1943, 210-211.

first of the Apostles as they bestow upon him a universal primacy that the Catholic tradition celebrates in a hundred different ways. In a letter to Pope Cornelius, and with an allusion to the Church of Rome, St. Cyprian writes that the pope is "the matrix and root of the Catholic Church."[9] In a different letter (but addressed to the same pope) he refers to Peter's chair and the principal Church "from which sacerdotal unity arises."[10] St. Ambrose's thought is no different: "The Roman Church is the head of the whole Roman world."[11]

The relationship between St. Peter and the pope is similar to, indeed is one with, the relation of derivation that we have just treated. Protestant theologians prefer not to acknowledge this relationship for fear that it might almost mean that Christ has invested Peter with a personal prerogative (Cullmann).

We accept an unshaken Catholic tradition that finds in Leo the Great (to cite but one) a distinguished and authoritative witness as he defines the pope: "prince of the apostolic order."[12] Here we notice another relationship, which we may characterize as that of brotherhood on the one hand, and on the other of pre-eminence not only in honor but in authority as well. This is very well known; and so is the pre-eminence of the pope over all the faithful.

It is the pope just recently deceased who reminds us of this in those memorable words with which he announced his intention of convening an ecumenical council. "Well," exclaims John XXIII, "venerable brothers and beloved children, in

9. St. Cyprian, *Eph.*, 48, 3 in Budé, II, p. 118: *Ecclesiae catholicae matricem et radicem.*
10. St. Cyprian, *Eph.*, 59, 14, 1 in Budé, II, p. 183: *unde unitas sacerdotalis exorta est.*
11. St. Ambrose, *Eph.*, 11, 4: *Totius orbis Romani caput Romanam Ecclesiam.*
12. St. Leo, *Serm.*, 82, 3: *Princeps apostolici ordinis.* Cf. G. Corti, *Pietro . . . Scuola Cattolica*, 1956, pp. 5 and 6.

thinking over the two-fold task entrusted to St. Peter's successor, we immediately notice his two-fold responsibility, as bishop of Rome and as pastor of the universal Church. Two expressions are embodied in one sole superhuman investiture; two functions that cannot be separated, that must indeed be joined in order to encourage and edify both the clergy and the entire laity."[13]

The raising of the pope not only to the center but to the summit as well both moves and intoxicates the Church, as the christian sensibility praises him with such sublime and solemn names as holiness, supreme pontiff, venerable, sovereign head of the Church, vicar of Christ, rock of faith and representative of the whole Church.[14] These names do not signify that the pope derives his functions from the Church, but rather that he sums up in his person the full powers of the whole Church. At the same time the pope is known by more human and more familiar names. Pope means father, and he is the shepherd, the servant of the servants of God.

The pope's position is, to be sure, so exalted and so singular that we should like to see it defined with the utmost precision. And this is exactly what the Vatican Council has done in defining the pope's privileges in terms that are by now dogmatic, that is, certain and indisputable and that may be summed up in the following three terms: primacy, infallibility, indefectibility.

These definitions are worth mentioning in the light of Part One of the First Dogmatic Constitution. This constitution is called first because it deals with the papacy while the second constitution that was to have dealt with the episcopacy and the laity was never discussed, since Vatican Council I was interrupted by the events of September 20, 1870. The first constitution emerged from the fourth session of the Vatican Council on July 18, 1870, under the

13. *A.A.S.*, 1959, 66.
14. St. Augustine, *Eph.*, 53, 1, 2: *Totius Ecclesiae figuram gerens.*

title derived from the opening words, "Pastor aeternus." The following ample and lucid prologue is worth citing:

The Eternal Pastor and Bishop of our souls (cf. 1 Pt 2: 25), in order to continue for all time the life-giving work of his redemption, determined to build up the holy Church, wherein, as in the house of the living God, all who believe might be united in the bond of one faith and one charity. Wherefore, before he entered into his glory, he prayed unto the Father, not for the Apostles only, but for those also who through their preaching should come to believe in him, that all might be one even as he the Son and the Father are one (cf. Jn 17).

As then he sent the Apostles whom he had chosen to himself from the world, as he himself had been sent by the Father: so he willed that there should ever be pastors and teachers in his Church to the end of the world. And in order that the episcopate also might be one and undivided, and that by means of a closely united priesthood the multitude of the faithful might be kept secure in the oneness of faith and communion, he set blessed Peter over the rest of the Apostles, and fixed in him the abiding principle of this two-fold unity, and its visible foundation, in the strength of which the everlasting temple should arise and the Church in the firmness of that faith should lift her majestic front to heaven.

And seeing that the gates of hell with daily increase of hatred are gathering their strength on every side to upheave the foundation laid by God's own hand, and so, if that might be, to overthrow the Church: we, therefore, for the preservation, safekeeping, and increase of the Catholic flock, with the approval of the sacred Council, do judge it to be necessary to propose to the belief and acceptance of all the faithful, in accordance with the ancient and constant faith of the universal Church, the doctrine touching the institution, perpetuity, and nature of the sacred apostolic primacy, in which is found the strength and solidity of the entire Church, and at the same time to proscribe and condemn the contrary errors, so hurtful to the flock of Christ.[15]

We therefore teach and declare that, according to the testimony of the Gospel, the primacy of jurisdiction over the universal Church of God was immediately and directly promised and given to blessed Peter the Apostle by Christ the Lord.[16]

15. Denzinger, 1821.
16. Denzinger, 1822.

The canons that follow declare that Peter is the visible head of the entire Church militant, endowed with primacy of jurisdiction, and that he finds perpetual successors in the Roman pontiffs, who are likewise vested with jurisdiction over the entire Church and with ordinary and immediate powers over each single church as well as each single pastor and layman. Finally, they declare that Christ has vested Peter with an infallibility that he has passed on to his successors in so far as they define doctrines regarding matters of faith and morals "ex cathedra," that is, in so far as they discharge their apostolic office of pastor and teacher in virtue of their supreme authority.[17]

But if this definition convinces, reassures and as a matter of fact consoles us Catholics, it produces no such effect on those who are not fortunate enough to live within the Catholic Church.

The Pope's Authority

Unity entails two consequences that our dissident brothers, precisely because they are separated, do not wish to admit. The one is exclusiveness and the other obedience.

But unity is not to be identified with either promiscuity or multiplicity, for the very moment that it asserts and determines itself it likewise distinguishes and defines itself. Unity separates those who conform from those who do not. Hence the unity of Catholics seems to be an exclusive concept, or better an exclusive program for religious life. This is the reason why Christ said that he himself came to bring the sword and not peace.

"The supposition that there could be several independent Christian societies with a 'spiritual unity' is 'totally alien to the thought of St. Paul,' "[18] and contrary to the whole of the

17. Denzinger, 1823; 1825; 1831; 1840.
18. Armitage Robinson, *Ephesians*, 2nd ed., p. 93; Joseph Huby, *Saint Paul, Epitres de la Captivité*, p. 196.

history of primitive Christianity."[19] Thus unity involves obedience: that is, conformity to an order established by competent authority. Unity and authority are correlative, as are unity and obedience. This is a harsh word for those who have not learned how to penetrate the divine economy of the Church as it is realized in human weakness.

Some have argued that this economy is impossible. The Chancellor of the University of Paris, later bishop and cardinal of Cambrai, Pierre d'Ailly, who played a great role in the councils of Pisa and Constance, believed it unlikely that the Lord should have established "the strength of Christ's Church on weakness," and that it was rather the case that Christ established the Church's stability by giving the weak Simon of Jonah the strength of a rock.

Others have argued against the excessive power the Church vests in the pope. And it was precisely in order to avoid the recognition of such a power that contemporary liberal Protestants have maintained that the Church is no visible and hierarchical society but solely a spiritual and invisible one, though in doing so they have failed to note that it is not simply the Roman Catholic Church but the very Church itself that becomes thereby dissolved.

Father Louis Bouyer, the distinguished French theologian and writer and convert from Protestantism, has expressed this idea in a forceful statement "based on a formula of St. Ignatius of Antioch, 'an invisible Church is the same thing as no Church at all'; without a hierarchy which is its point of crystallization, its organizer and its guide, 'there can be no talk of the Church.' "[20]

A despotic, imperialist and politicizing kind of papacy is so feared that, in order to withhold obedience from it the unity of the Church, of the true Church, comes to be sacri-

19. Henri de Lubac, *The Splendor of the Church* (New York: Sheed and Ward, 1956), p. 57.
20. Quoted in de Lubac, *op. cit.*, p. 58.

ficed. But how can we answer an objection that has raised such a formidable obstacle against the movement towards unity? This is not an obstacle of the sort that can be removed by a facile apologetical argument.

We shall simply say that the fear of obeying an arbitrary and tyrannical power is absolutely unfounded. Obedience, to be sure, does involve humility and fidelity, patience and sacrifice. Yet it is neither unreasonable if willed by Christ nor unlimited if restricted to one specific sphere of competence. Neither is it alien to the good of those who profess it since it actually guarantees and protects that good. Still less is it remote and motivated by reasons that are intrinsic to the believer's very soul.

Let us listen to the words of his excellency Monsignor Blanchet, rector of the Institut Catholique of Paris:

When the Pope makes an act of doctrinal authority, this is no exterior yoke which a particular man imposes on a religious society in the name of his own intelligence, even though it might be that of a genius. He is defining the faith of the Church. He is in no way subject to her consent; yet the truth which he translates into our language and renders precise is the truth by which she lives; the belief whose meaning he confirms is our belief—he analyses its content, counters its potential weakenings and maintains its vigour. Thus, when we say to the Church, in the words which the Apostle used to Christ, who founded her: 'To whom shall we go? Thou has the words of eternal life,' this is not in virtue of some fatigue of spirit which seeks to place itself under an authority to escape the effort of thought and the labour of living; rather it is, as Newman put it, in virtue of a sense of coming to rest in the Catholic plenitude.[21]

Let us now invoke the testimony of such a representative man as Newman, and recall his prayer in this respect: "May I, O Lord, never forget for one instant that Thou hast established a kingdom on this earth that belongs to Thee, that the Church is Thy work, Thy foundation, Thy instrument, that

21. Msgr. Blanchet, as quoted by de Lubac, *op. cit.*, p. 201.

we are under Thy guidance, Thy laws, Thy gaze, and that when the Church speaks, it is Thee who is speaking."[22]

And let us recall the testimony of another wise man, this time a man from the East, Soloviev. In moving from Orthodoxy to Catholicism, he makes the following confession: "The perfect circle of the universal Church needs one single center, not in order to be perfect but simply in order to remain a real society. The terrestrial Church, called to embrace the multitude of nations, had to oppose a distinct universal power against all national divisions."[23]

Let us recall the experience we have all had of the papacy in recent years. Providence has blessed us with one great fortune, that of providing us with a vicar of Christ who is no longer burdened with any terrestrial sovereignty, unless we mean to refer to the surviving fringe of land that is certainly useless as an instrument of power and is but a tiny though unmistakable symbol of independence and freedom. Today Christ's vicar is completely absorbed in discharging his evangelical mission: first of all to teach, to reawaken in men a knowledge of divine principles, to enlighten and infuse them with trust in human thought and to indicate to society the ways of social evolution; to admonish rulers and nations of encroaching errors and imminent dangers and to judge events and doctrines in the light of eternal values.

For decades the teaching of the popes has been proclaimed within the Church as never before, and proclaimed openly to the whole world.

Other objects of the evangelical mission must be noted: to guide Christ's flock and arouse from the Church's inmost depths the energies and works through which it gains its vitality and splendor. With these it fires its children with a zeal to do good and emulate every sane conquest and provident activity, for it is not the world that furnishes the Church

22. Cf. *ibid.*, p. 195.
23. Vladimir Soloviev, *Russia and the Universal Church*, p. 183.

with its vitality and splendor. Another object is to reopen a dialogue, a fresh dialogue with the world of culture and art, with a civilization that is saturated with techniques yet ignorant of ends. Again, to sanctify God's Church by accelerating the circulation of grace within it, by reawakening in its ranks a sense of and relish for prayer and charity, and by suggesting fresh ways to sanctity.

In recent years, in the confusion of nations at war, we have seen the Pope speak out alone and preach peace; we have seen him bend over every human wound and make his evangelical message merge with the deepest exigencies of human life: goodness, justice, mercy, freedom, the dignity of the human person, life itself. Almost always isolated and neglected, yet in his very position detached from all worldly interests, alien to every human competition, a frequent target of inexplicable and bitter attacks, we have seen him stand out alone, a unique phenomenon in the midst of mankind, almost as if he were a point of reference and convergence, surrounded by a strange and universal presentiment that the destiny of civilization would revolve around him. It is not that the pope has access to wealth, means, force and power. Something quite different is involved: he is sympathetic to every human need and repelled by every human injustice, and he has the courage necessary to sustain every ideal principle. Finally, he possesses the humility and dignity of the man of God.

The papacy rises above the world through the prophetic gifts of those who preach the gospel and proclaim a hope that transcends the boundaries of time.

To Construct Unity

If the world paid greater attention to this spiritual reality, it would spare itself many "useless stratagems." It would direct its many deviant efforts towards profitable ends and would correct its many unworthy acts for its own honor and peace of mind.

And if those who still turn to Christ as the world's salvation possessed a more intimate knowledge of the religious doctrines and forms of life that govern the papacy, they would not allow themselves to be scandalized by the many historical events of the past in which many churchmen made a dismal showing through their human weakness, any more than they would be impressed by certain contingent and questionable phases of the Roman chronicle. They would rather be astonished and rejoice to see how Christ's mystery lives in him who is called the vicar of Christ. If, as we were saying, those who still turn to Christ as the world's salvation were to view with a serene eye the papacy's real essence and real activity rather than dwell on the often reiterated separation between spiritual and corporeal christianity (Luther), between the visible and the invisible Church (Calvin), between the religion of authority and the religion of the spirit (Sabatier), between the Church of law and the Church of love, the Church as institution and the Church as event, the hierarchical Church and the charismatic Church, they would realize how wrong and unjust it is to turn these distinctions into real antinomies and apply them, especially today, to the Roman pontificate. For on the contrary, it is precisely because it is the Church's highest expression, the juridical, that the papacy is the most faithful custodian and the most generous power of Christ's word, charity and grace throughout christendom and the whole world.[24]

This is what we believe, we who are so often intolerant in our criticism of the papacy, so often saturated with the self-sufficient dogmatism that is the mark of a closed mentality and so quick therefore to see its defects and disallow its merits; we who are so greatly prejudiced against the sup-

24. Cf. Pope Pius XII, *A.A.S.*, 1943, 250; also *Mystici Corporis*, *ibid.*, 223-224.

posed reactionary attitudes of the Roman Curia yet are hardly eager to comply with the directives that the pope issues to us for the christian regeneration of society. Thus if we were not too distracted by everything which that seat of truth and goodness has so generously bestowed upon us, and if we had a more trustful and pious sense of Christ and his Church, if our desire for peace among men and our love for unity among christians were more sincere and more ardent, we would experience a new birth and a new strength in our hearts. We would experience a feeling that has remained dormant and too often uncertain; we would experience the "Catholic" feeling: the consciousness of the human universality that is achieved through our freedom as God's children. We would also be conscious of a unity that is spiritual and in some mysterious way real, that is fixed in a center that focuses Christ's design and is concretized in one person, his vicar the pope, while at the same time it widens out into an immense circle that longs to become one with the whole world. We would decidedly not be conscious of this "Catholic" feeling for the sake of realizing a dream of arrogance and domination, but rather for the sake of fulfilling a duty of communion and equality. We are not speaking of a dream but of a firm intention and pledge of an apostolic charity that is anxious to share the name of brother with every man and help every man partake of the heritage of truth and grace that, through no merit of ours, we yet have the fortune and the responsibility to possess. We must, in short, work to build unity.

To build unity! To labor for the building of Catholic unity! Why should this not occur, when the whole world is agitated by a need for union and peace among men, when temporal society itself yearns for the world's unification and seems open to the Gospel, when the Church exhorts each one of us, its children, and urges us to serve as missionaries and apostles within our own society that is gradually losing the christian spirit and christian morals? Why should this not occur when a pope, gentle and wise, announces the convocation of that tribunal of unity which is the Ecumenical Council, and invites all of us to prepare ourselves for it and celebrate the happy event by prayer and charity?

With this reawakened Catholic consciousness, why shouldn't we—all of us—prepare ourselves in some way to build unity? And should this come about in fact, we would see ourselves transformed into "builders," into laborers for unity; we would see, under our own eyes and under our own hands, the shaping of the building's marvellous design. And we would hear in our souls an echo of the Divine Architect's prophetic words: "thou art Peter, and it is upon this rock that I will build my church" (Mt 16: 18).

We say all this precisely because there can be no true religious unity without the Church, and no true Church without the papacy.

What the Church Is and What the Church Is Not

We Must Understand the Church Anew

My brethren and fellow believers!

I have been assigned the task of introducing the great theme that will engage our attention throughout this Mission, whose main preoccupation is to reawaken the religious and spiritual life of our city. Our theme is "The Church our mother."

This introduction has been conceived as a choice between two roads that lead in different directions so that we may find the right road at the very outset, and leave aside the misleading paths that might take us beyond our intended goal.

We must find our bearings at once and learn "what the Church is and what it is not," for this is the exact theme of this simple introduction. Though presented in this two-fold proposition, it is a theme that is nonetheless one, for its aim, in substance, is to furnish us with a true concept of the Church, about which we shall later talk at length.

It is of interest to note that the topic has been proposed under the form of an alternative and indeed of a conflict, an opposition. This reveals at once a fact of great importance:

the fact that it is possible to entertain conflicting judgments about the Church. And experience does in fact bear this out repeatedly.

The existence of many conflicting judgments does not depend solely on the manifold complexity of the Church. Let this observation suffice for the moment as a caution against any longer enunciating hasty and summary opinions about the Church, for we usually fail in this honest precaution and risk pronouncements that distort our own understanding of this majestic fact called the Church.

The Church's complex character is by no means the sole source of the multiple judgments about it, for these judgments are often rooted in the different states of mind through which the Church is viewed. It is easy for us to shape our definition of the Church on the basis of the subjective conditions of our minds for we are eager to cast it in either a favorable or an unfavorable light, depending on our own particular circumstances.

Let this be the first objective then of your Mission, and the specific purpose of my introduction: let us understand the Church anew. This need was not as sharply felt when people habitually lived in the Church and made its thought and morals their own. But now the Church has become the object of contention and, in practice at least, has been banished from the modern mind, from the secular conception of life. Hence, if we wish to regain entry consciously, or at least justify for our own satisfaction our reasons for abandoning the ancient paternal home, we must form for ourselves a more reflective, precise and essential idea of the Church. And this need is no less serious and no less urgent for those of us who are fortunate enough to be still living serenely in the spiritual home of our ancestors.

The Catholic tradition itself demands that we become conscious of it. A great many stimuli create this need even for the Catholic believer. One of the chief stimulations arises from the exhaustive studies of the origins of christianity: is the Church of today the same as the Church in its original form? And if so, will it always be the same?

Then the controversy—ever more interesting even though today more serene and gracious—between the Catholic Church and the various separated churches makes the problem alive and timely: which is the true Church? and where does it realize its true idea?

And the distinction, ever more pronounced, between the ecclesiastical and the civil society raises the question of the relations between church and state. Whereas in the Middle Ages there was one sole concept of society, christendom as governed by two powers, today we think of two societies as separate and sovereign yet by necessity sharing the same citizens. And we ask ourselves what is the nature of this Church that is so exacting as to compete against the state not simply as a religion claiming a free profession of its own beliefs but as a true social body, organic and independent in character.

Moreover we might say that today the idea of the Church that Jesus Christ conceived and established, instead of becoming weaker and more impoverished because of the emergence of conceptions that contest its legitimate existence, and because of the subsequent oppressions and persecutions that were aimed at suffocating its existence—the idea of the Church is gaining ground as it goes about arousing a new interest in a number of religious people. And in fact it is these religious people who are engaged in working out a theology of the Church through new and exhaustive studies such as had not yet ripened throughout the age-old development of Catholic doctrine. And these same religious people are also becoming aware of the fact that the Church, usually considered merely in its external—historical and social—form, is at the same time a marvellous kingdom in which the inner life may flourish. For it is precisely in this inner kingdom that those who know how to see and discern may discover, and to a certain degree experience, the wonderful process in which the divine and human elements meet.

And so this Mission shows how responsive it is to modern trends of thought and how profitable it can be for a religious revival, both spiritual and pastoral.

Yet the fact remains that the concept of the Church that is common and widespread is neither univocal nor incontestable nor clear. The Church is a target attacked for its contradictions just as Christ was, *signum cui contradicetur*, "a sign which men will refuse to acknowledge" (Lk 2: 34). The Church is a problem. And here we face a strange phenomenon indeed. The Church that ought to be and in fact is the *signum elevatum in nationes*, "the standard high lifted, for a world to see" (Is 11: 12), the standard raised in the midst of peoples so as to show the field of our salvation, the Church that is defined as "the pillar and foundation upon which the truth rests" (1 Tim 3: 15) and is marked by the four notes that characterize the authenticity of the Catholic religion—this Church constitutes for many people an obstacle to faith and a scandal for the religious world, though this scandal, let us note, is conceived in the light of a superficial yet frequently sincere and modern spiritual vision. Why this difficulty? Why this ambiguity?

Corrupt Aspects That Fail to Define the Church's Reality

Before answering, let us survey very rapidly those aspects that most commonly show the Church as it is not. As it is not in its essence, function, finality—that is to say, in its inmost and to a large extent invisible reality. For the corrupt aspects themselves are unfortunately real, or at least present an appearance that is undeniable, though not such as to define the Church's true and total reality.

In reading Christ's thought St. Paul presents an image of supreme beauty in which he describes the Church almost as if it were the whole of mankind so transfigured and ideal as to merit Christ's love, almost as if it were a bride, beautiful and glorious, unstained and free of all imperfection, holy and immaculate (cf. Eph 5: 27).

But, asks the observer who is not accustomed to contemplate the Church's profound truth, where is he to find this beauty, where is he to find this splendor of the Church that history in the concrete fails to display?

You Florentines undoubtedly remember those literary documents that stigmatize certain types of churchmen with a mordant mockery, and you know that these types have remained unfortunately famous. In this respect it is enough to recall the classical invectives of father Dante that you all know so well.

One of the most frequent distortions of the Church's resplendent and regal countenance is furnished precisely by many of its own members—and unfortunately, even by its own representatives on occasion. The literature of the last century, for example, amused itself with what became as it were a set theme: that of the priest, unworthy of his mission and degenerate in his vocation—unwittingly perhaps—who embodies and serves evil so effectively that he disgraces his vocation by the incurable taint of ridicule.

But when the priest and the believer appear in the literature of our day the picture is different, for the man of the Church is now idealized and portrayed as he ought to be. And once again our literary writers make us believe that the real priest is inferior to the ideal one. They engender in us, even though unwittingly, a certain distrust of the real man of the Church who in the concrete might disappoint us and fail to be all that he is expected to be: namely, a man of inner depth, magnanimous, heroic, humble, detached, loving. And even when our contemporary writers and artists do accentuate some positive trait in a priest, they seem to take special pains to note that the trait in question is not specifically

religious and that it does not enter into any of the characteristic features of Catholic life that are, as they say, clerical.
Apart from literature and the theater, the anti-clerical mentality has become at times so entrenched and widespread
among persons and institutions related to the Church, and
in a country officially Catholic such as Italy, that it becomes
transformed outright into a hostile prejudice.

The great and tragic events of the two wars had shaken
this prejudice, but immediately thereafter partisan minds
arose to revive and consolidate it again, so that the atmosphere of our public life is still impregnated with an instinc-
tive distrust of the Church and a collective humanistic respect
that on occasion even enjoys official sanction. We are surrounded on all sides by a fashionable antipathy against all
that has to do with religious and ecclesiastical matters, or at
most by an indulgence born of good manners rather than of
a serene and sympathetic disposition that acknowledges the
right and the merit of all that has to do with a Church which
it both esteems and trusts.

I cannot say that the men and things that have to do with
the Church are free of blame. On the contrary I myself
would be tempted to deplore the deficiencies, culpable or
not, of the clergy.

To call attention to the disproportion between the Church's
human reality and the ideal that it ought to realize causes
a persistent and burning sorrow in those who love the
Church and in those who hold responsible positions in it.
I frequently feel uneasy, and suffer, when I observe that at
times it is we men of the Church who furnish a pretext and
a reason for the hostility against the Church and religion on
the part of men who perhaps lack education yet are ready to
judge spiritual values summarily by the way in which the
clergy and Catholics in general embody them.

On occasion this hostility arises even in people who are
educated, and who instinctively expect religious men and

religious circles to project an image that is worthy of so exacting a profession. And it is these same people who are frequently scandalized when they find themselves confronted with a vision that is pitifully unworthy of all that christian reality ought to be.

Thus I feel that it is my duty to beg pardon of the many people who are annoyed, and of the many unbelievers who are separated from either God or Christ and remain hostile to the Church because we men, men of the Church, have neither furnished them, in a worthy manner, with the ideal that is our distinguishing mark, nor have known how to earn their esteem and trust.

Instead of being a channel for the truth of faith and a mirror of christian virtue for these people, it is quite possible that I have been an opaque screen and a troublesome obstacle.

Mea culpa!

Contemporary thinkers have seen the phenomenon on a large scale and have shown that one of the causes of modern apostasy is a deep rooted resentment against a christian world that is unworthy of its principles, "and not only against the christian world (and here lies the tragedy) but against christianity itself" (cf. Maritain, Berdyaev, etc.). Yes, I shall have to consider this responsibility in all humility and seriousness, yet I shall feel no shame in begging the pardon of the men of my age if I have failed to furnish them with a fresh and living image of the Church's reality, or with the treasury of truth that it teaches me, or with some experience of its goodness and of the grace that it ministers to me.

And I, in turn, shall urge the men of my age to be what they themselves claim to be when they assume a critical and hostile position: namely, intelligent.

Very often those who claim to be so are not really scandalized. The old answer to this formidable and persistent objection against the Church remains valid, and is forever worthy precisely of intelligent men: let us learn to distinguish the person from the office, the minister from the ministry.

Moreover, this intellectual exercise whereby we distinguish the man from the office should raise no difficulty whatsoever since we are compelled to live it out day after day in our advanced and highly organized society. And even if it should be more difficult to apply this distinction in the religious sphere because the men who preach the holy life ought to be holy and the men who preach Christ ought to be authentic christians by virtue of a certain inner exigency of fidelity and integrity and even efficacy, nevertheless the distinction is by no means unjustified. On the contrary, in conformity with the essence of the christian economy, let us recall St. Augustine's great polemic and the many controversies originating with him in this respect: the validity of supernatural grace does not depend on those who dispense it, but solely on Christ. The distinction is also in harmony with the cultural maturity of our age that acknowledges the greatness, the perennial greatness of the religious fact, even when it is overcome with humiliation on the one hand, and on the other demands that those who approach it be humble.

The Church Is Not an Ancient, Conservative Institution

Yet this is not all. The antipathy toward the clergy is not the only way in which the Church's radiant countenance is disfigured; there are many other disfigurements that show us what the Church is not. Let us survey some of them briefly.

There is a kind of antipathy for the Church that is engendered within the spirit of modern man as he accuses it of being an ancient institution, an organism belonging to another age and one that has had its day. Moreover, it is extremely conservative. Its scrupulous fidelity to the past causes it to drag along a chain that is heavy enough for those within the Church, and heavier still for those who have cut themselves loose from the Church though they continue to feel its weight.

Tradition is inconceivable for those ages born of revolution, that is, of a repudiation of the past and its useless heritage. Modern man looks to the present and the future rather than to the past as the Church does, and is in fact obliged to do. The persistence of such an organism in our own age is, modern man believes, a case of obscurantism and ultra-conservatism. And it is at this point that the modern mind springs forth to decree that the time has come to render the Church outmoded by applying our intellectual powers to the positive and natural sciences, by fostering a technological and industrial spirit among men, by unleashing anti-religious sentiments within contemporary social and political movements, and by an escape from metaphysics and a suspicion of all logical certitude.

It is impossible, we are told, for a modern man to understand the Church.

Those who still retain some respect for man's past activities reduce the Church to a simple historical phenomenon, to a moment in the evolution of civilization, to a respectable relic fit to be relegated to treatises on mythology and archeology and to be viewed in our museums. They treat the Church with the same indulgence that they display toward the dead; the same indulgence for this, the living Church!

Let us submit just two observations concerning this manner of judging the Church as if its human countenance were marked by the wretched features of a cruel old age, if not by the altogether cadaverous sickliness of an uninvited ghost. That is to say, we would never pass this sort of judgment on the Church if we possessed a wiser and more refined sense of history. And we indulge these extravagant fantasies about the Church's old age, about its outmoded futility in the contemporary world, because the ways of contemporary thought have been dominated by the revolutionary and irresponsible spirit that is so pervasive today. It does our culture no honor to characterize the tradition that the Church indomitably guards as a dead weight for the modern spirit; on the contrary, it prevents us from building something solid, coherent and sensitive to the new civilization.

In the second place, it is entirely wrong to believe that the Church is simply a survival from the past, a creature of time; that just as time has brought it to birth so will it eventually devour it; and that, furthermore, it is a history that looks backward and treasures its centuries old past as its sole title to glory. This belief, we say, is entirely wrong, not only because the Church bears eternity as a living reality and displays an everlasting youth and vitality that do not originate in this world, but because it is wrong to believe that the Church is turned only towards the past.

The Church is, to be sure, fixed to its twin source, Christ and the Gospel. It is inserted in both time and history, and bears that event and moment in time that we know as the God-man's redemptive mission on earth. Yet at the same time it stretches out toward the future, toward the future return of the glorious Christ. It reaches out toward its eschatological destiny, as it is put. It lives on the past, but in the present and for the future: its hope is its strength. And its special and constitutional nature makes it forever self-consistent, forever responsive in adapting itself to contemporary problems, forever ancient and forever modern.

Surely this will take place neither without effort nor opposition, for such is the mark of human affairs, even though they be guided by superhuman principles. But what we must assert at the moment is the Church's right to remain at one and the same time eternally faithful and eternally youthful. And since the Church is composed of men and for men, nobody in and by himself is a stranger, nobody an enemy, for the Church belongs to everybody virtually and is capable of adapting itself to all who are joined to it through faith.

The Church Does Not Teach an Aprioristic, Incomprehensible, Indisputable, Rigid Doctrine

There is yet something else, more serious and more difficult to explain, that we find as we seek to help our contemporaries understand and love the Church's face as a mother's. What they perceive rather than a lovable and lively expression is a face that is rigid, a face that is like marble, motionless and speechless. Yet this is precisely the countenance that the Church claims for itself. It is the countenance of one teaching a dogmatic doctrine, a doctrine that our age calls aprioristic, incomprehensible, indisputable and rigid.

This is its reality, its peremptory and opaque face according to those who claim to have penetrated the Church's true character. It is for this reason that we men of culture, we sons of freedom, we who profess systematic doubt, we eternal searchers, dissatisfied and uneasy, cannot accept the Church.

The aversion to ecclesiastical dogmatism drives secular thought to the opposite extreme. People say—and try to act accordingly—that the Church's doctrinal intransigeance will result in its being excluded from the world of thought, of education, of science, of progress. Here the gap seems unbridgeable, the opposition unanswerable. Yet at least theoretically, this pseudo-vision of the Church is easier to correct than any other, because according to the Church's dogmatism error has no reason to exist for all men who love truth.

If the Church's dogmas are true and express realities; if they are contained within the sphere of thoroughly meditated concepts and thoroughly examined formulations, so that they deny nothing that is certain and affirm nothing that is uncertain, why then should we renounce them? It will be difficult to prove that these assertions are true, but if they should turn out to be so, why then should the man of culture, the man of thought, reject them?

Would not he himself then be prey to a priori conceptions?

And if those truths were not supported by internal evidence but rather by the evidence of an authorized and honest teaching body would they have to be rejected? On this point too it will not be easy to establish that the magisterium is in fact authorized by divine institution. But if it were established, as it in fact is, why then reject it? And if it does give us some knowledge, some revelation that we would be unable to gain by ourselves, why should we deprive ourselves of such a contribution of knowledge and light?

Would we not then be the obscurantists?

This is an old and much debated question, complex and delicate, yet not without a positive solution. We need not labor what matters most: dogmas are neither arbitrary nor dead concepts, but living truths. We need only ask honestly if the teaching Church really is an obstacle to culture, thought, scholarship and science when the facts reveal the complete opposite. Today, on the contrary, it seems that it is precisely Catholic schools that defend the power of thought, and foster both a passion for humanistic knowledge and an ardent respect for scientific research. And it is in this fashion that Catholic schools seek to sustain, within modern culture itself, a consciousness, a confidence, a zeal that we feel threatened by contemporary materialistic and existentialistic currents.

Who still believes in truth today? Who will defend us from the vertigo of the absurd that many believe to be the last word of human thought? Who will disillusion us of those utopias that narcotize the thought that questions its own principles?

In the midst of the widespread intellectual and moral apathy of our age, poisoned as it were by boredom and sensuality, who will teach us to discover an unobtrusive suffering, a restrained sigh, a desperate hope for redemption and love? The austere gaze of the teaching Church once again encompasses mankind, clouded and obstructed in its vision, and enlightens it with powers of new and undreamed of visions.

We have not thereby exhausted the images of the Church, for they are innumerable. We shall consider but one, though it might well turn out to be the most disconcerting of all. According to this image the Church is nothing less than Christ's disfigurement.

The contrast between the Church and the figure of its founder has been enormously successful in the anti-clerical controversy. The contrast has its origin in a certain puritanism, a certain passion for christian sources, a certain intolerance for some of the concrete forms of the Church's life.

The objection is two-fold. One is doctrinal, and accuses the Church of having altered the genuine evangelical message through its theological speculation (this charge is still made against scholastic intellectualism). The other is moral, and denounces the Church's moral failures and political mistakes.

The comparison between certain churchmen and Christ the Lord has seemed at times to justify this denigrating theory. Let us recall, for example, the Little Brothers whom John XXII condemned (Denz., 485). When the decay of christian morals was held up to the evangelical ideal, it did lend frequent support to this severe criticism of the Church. The Protestant Reformation capitalized vigorously on the abuses for which it held the Catholic Church responsible. Then came the literary men—we all remember Tolstoi who took issue with all the churches as if they were anti-christian institutions that represented, in his opinion, "Satan's revenge."

Yet what can we say about the many evils that did unfortunately exist in the Church? Can we deny them? Can we misrepresent their gravity? Can we justify them? No, this we cannot do. On the contrary, we must be sincere and face reality squarely, especially historical reality, for this we can judge more openly and objectively. Nor can we alter historical reality simply because we love the Church.

Yet we must reflect, especially in reference to the contemporary scene, about the Gospel's injunction against our judging men in the light of those supreme responsibilities that make them good or evil in the eyes of God. In this respect we are not competent. Before we give a truthful and serene judgment even in a purely historical context, we must acquire a complete knowledge of the environment. Furthermore, we must remember that in our age the criticism of the Church has become intense, especially in terms of the historical and doctrinal development of the Church's privileges.

"The more thoroughly a Church develops a theory of its own powers (some will say, of its own claims) the more severely will it be criticized. . . . This is the background of that famous anti-Roman complex that is among the strongest and most diligently sustained feelings in non-Catholic countries" (Congar). In addition, Catholics themselves have become more intolerant of the weaknesses they encounter in the Church, and no longer wish to defend it in such a form. In fact, the self-criticism of Catholics is excessive at times, and the tendency today is to blame the Church itself for very many evils that powerful adversaries have inflicted on it.

But let me repeat, what are we to say? Above all we shall say that the Catholic Church itself is the first to acknowledge and condemn its own faults, and that it has never claimed to be perfect on earth. On the contrary, it never ceases to reproach itself for its own faults, to preach penance for itself, to acknowledge the frailty of its own members and to foster a continual reform of itself.

And let nobody say that in this effort the Church ever betrays its divine model, Christ crucified.

Secondly, if we wish to discover the Church's true features, we shall say that we must look more intently at its countenance, often besmirched and wounded. We must look more deeply.

The Church Is a Mystery

Let us now return to the question we mentioned before. How on earth has the Church come to display such an ambiguous and incomprehensible appearance? How on earth can the Church so easily appear to be what it is not? Because *Ecclesia ex hominibus*, the Church is composed of men. "Again, the kingdom of heaven is like a net that was cast into the sea, and enclosed fish of every kind at once" (Mt 13: 47): good and bad, pure and impure, ancient and modern, barbarian and Greek.

Then there are those with myopic vision who, no longer scandalized by the weaker aspects of the Church's human countenance, become blinded by its higher aspects. Transfixed in enchantment, they behold its earthly grandeur, its civilizing power, its greco-roman treasure and its artistic flowering. All these features are certainly real, yet they express a reality that is phenomenal in character and hence fails to reveal the Church's true and profound reality, its inmost essence and soul.

For the Church does have a soul, which is to say that the Church is a mystery.

Yes, the Church is a mystery. This word raises a two-fold difficulty that explains our perplexity and confusion with regard to the Church. First is the difficulty of a study that aims at penetrating the true nature of this great and mysterious organism, that does not shrink from the effort required to gain knowledge and to think, and is not devoid of a heart-felt reverence, gratitude and hope.

Secondly, I speak of the difficulty that in itself is mysterious, of a grace that opens our eyes and bestows upon us this marvellous vision.

The Church is a truth of faith and faith, in its inmost and primordial splendor, is grace; it is God's favor.

Here we enter into God's over-arching plan for the world, a plan that is known to us only in fragments and as it affects the history of our salvation.

We might in fact know everything about the Church yet not really understand it: *videntes non vident et audientes non audiunt,* as Christ says: "though they have eyes, they cannot see, and though they have ears, they cannot hear" (Mt 13: 13).

This two-fold difficulty explains why there will never be a concord of opinions and attitudes about the Church and warns us against becoming disheartened if we should see the Church misunderstood, ill judged and even treated more badly still. And here we confront one of the beatitudes: "Blessed are you, when men revile you, and persecute you, and speak all manner of evil against you falsely, because of me" (Mt 5: 11).

But right now, on this happy occasion, we are trying in some way to overcome this two-fold difficulty, and everything leads us to believe that we can succeed through the same act of good will that has brought us to this mission of salvation.

The Church is a mystery because it is a divine thought. "I will build my church," says Christ, architect of this immense human edifice (Mt 16: 18).

But what is his thought? And what is his design?

It springs, we answer, from the inmost depths of the divine wisdom. St. Paul warns us that this thought, that involves the salvation of mankind through the redemption of Christ, was a "mystery kept hidden from the beginning of time in the all-creating mind of God" (Eph 3: 9; Col 1: 26). It is in fact a luminous, marvellous and most joyful thought, a thought already in existence before it becomes embodied in history.

It is the city of God lowered from heaven, the heavenly Jerusalem embodied in the human clay that it illuminates, moulds and sanctifies, while forever remaining infinitely more beautiful and more perfect than any of its concrete and historical manifestations in time, in the inner depths of humanity.[1]

It is God's kingdom. It is the Church of God, the holy Church: an institutional reality, a conception essential and functional.

The Divine and Human Countenance of the Church, Mystical Body of Christ

Thus the Church presents two fundamental aspects. One mysterious, spiritual and divine displays the Church as an organism, enlivened by the Holy Spirit. Jesus infuses this Spirit in it, who bestows upon it the gifts and powers that sustain and guide, enliven and invigorate it, and make it worthy of being called holy, one and universal.

The other is visible and human, the *congregatio fidelium*. It is the assembly of believers that is ourselves as we constitute physically Christ's social body.

Both these aspects are precisely impressed in the two terms that together constitute St. Paul's classical formulation of what is the most synoptic and exact definition of the Church but that at the same time signify one sole reality: "Mystical Body."

This is exactly what the Church is: Christ's Mystical Body.[2] We should treasure this definition that Pope Pius XII

1. Cf. *Mystici Corporis, A.A.S.*, 1943, 219-220.
2. Cf. *ibid.*, 193-248; and cf. Tromp, *Textus et documenta*, p. 69ff.

makes so lucid and so relevant in his encyclical. It shows us "above all that the Church is at one and the same time spiritual and visible."

It is in fact truly spiritual, supernatural, "pneumatic," for its most important part—the essential, principal part of its being, its soul—is entirely spiritual, entirely supernatural.

Yet the Church is visible, absolutely speaking, *simpliciter*, for even its invisible soul is somehow made visible through the body that expresses its spiritual nature.[3]

We should pay special attention to this doctrinal point concerning the Church's spiritual and visible character since it marks a boundary line between us Catholics and those dissident christians, the first Reformers above all, who sought to escape the gravity of their claim that the medieval Church had crumbled and to mask the break between the Reformation and earlier centuries by counter-proposing the dogma that there is one sole Church, invisible, true, holy, completely spiritual and known to God alone.

In this fashion the mystery of the Incarnation would no longer be continued in the Church.

A great modern theologian, Scheeben, writes:

By becoming man the Son of God has called the whole human race to fellowship in His Body. That which was remote, that which was far from God and vastly below Him, He has brought near in His person, and has joined in one body, His own body. Upon Himself and in Himself He has established a great community and society of men. He is at once the head and the foundation of this society. In it He wills to continue His activity and His reign. Through it He wishes to unite men to Himself and to His heavenly Father. This society is the Church.

The Church is a great and stupendous mystery. It is a mystery in its very being, a mystery in its organization, a mystery in the power and activity it exercises . . .

When we assert that the Church is a mystery, do we intend to do away with its natural visibility? By no means; the Church is visible in its members, in its external organization, and in the

3.   Journet, *op. cit.*, II, p. 9.

relations existing between its superiors and subjects. It is as visible as any other human society.

I venture to make an even greater claim: the Church is visible not only as it actually stands at present, but in its divine foundation and institution . . .

The Church is visible in the very way that its historical founder and head, the God-man Himself, was visible.[4]

This doctrine shows us two of the Church's aspects, mysterious and visible, divine and human, and introduces us into a deeper knowledge of the Church's inmost nature, though to discuss this problem more fully would involve us in an endless meditation.

The various names given to the Church may be compared to a necklace of precious jewels. Let us begin with what we have been talking about: with the more common name "Church." That means assembly or convocation and already "manifests the generosity and splendor of divine grace and marks the distance that separates the Church from all other temporal realities."[5] This meaning suggests a call that concerns us, a responsibility that touches us, a grace that awaits us.

We should recall the scriptural names, and first of all the name of "kingdom," whose keys have been given to Peter, Christ's vicar: that is to say, the religion Christ founded, the divine economy established for the salvation of mankind.

We should speak of the "city" on the mountain (Mt 5: 14) and of the city of God that Pius IX identifies as Christ's Church (Denz., 1841).

We should explain how the Church comes to be the "communion of saints,"[6] why it is called "Christ's bride" (Eph 5: 23ff)[7] and is said to be "Christ's body";[8] why "God's

---

4. Matthias J. Scheeben, *The Mysteries of Christianity* (New York: Herder & Herder, 1946), pp. 539-540.
5. Journet, *op. cit.*, II, p. 50.
6. Cf. Piolanti, *Il mistero della Comunione dei Santi*, p. 11.
7. Journet, *op. cit.*, II, p. 112.
8. Cf. Tromp, *op. cit.*, p. 123.

house" (1 Tim 3: 15) and why "Jesus Christ's sacrament," that is, his mysterious continuation in history and in the world, his testimony and presence among us.[9]

Again, we should talk at length about the great name that is due to it, that of "teacher," and we should recall the beautiful names of "Christ's sheepfold," "Peter's boat," "God's people," "the land of christian hope."[10]

We should, for the sake of precision, cite one catechetical and classical definition, that of Bellarmine: "The Church is the society of journeying men, assembled by a profession of the same faith and through a participation in the same sacraments, under the guidance of the legitimate pastors and chiefly of the Roman Pontiff."[11]

These names point to a complex, magnificent and vital reality.

And it is this reality that causes St. John Chrysostom to exclaim: "Do not separate yourself from the Church. Nothing is stronger than it is. The Church is your hope, your refuge. It is higher than the heavens and wider than the earth. It never grows old; it is everlastingly young. . . . Scripture calls it a mountain . . . a virgin . . . a queen . . . and God's daughter . . . the Church may be called by a great many names."[12]

To Call the Church "Mother" Is to Understand It in a Fresh Way and Love It

You have already shown your preference for one of these names, that of mother. But why mother?

To penetrate the import of this name as it is referred to God's Church does indeed mean to understand it freshly,

9. Cf. de Lubac, *op. cit.*, p. 147ff., and Journet, II, p. 589.
10. Cf. *Cath. ad Parochos*, 1, 105.
11. St. Robert Bellarmine, *Controv. de Eccl. mil.*, 2.
12. St. John Chrysostom, *Hom. de Capto Eutropio*, 6.

to love it, to acknowledge its dignity, mission, goodness and necessity.

Mother, because the Church is the source of our life, of the true life that is the supernatural life, the life that will conquer death and reach a fullness of being.

The Church is bound to our destiny; or better still, it is we who are bound to it for our salvation. If Christ is our salvation it is the Church that gives it to us, for the Church gives us Christ. If God is life, it is the Church that obtains it for us.

Let us recall the celebrated words of St. Cyprian: "We cannot have God as Father unless we have the Church as mother."[13] Let us also recall the famous words of St. Augustine: "The christian must fear nothing more greatly than to be separated from Christ's body, for if he is separated from Christ's body he is no longer one of his members, and if he is not one of his members he is no longer quickened by his Spirit."[14]

It is the Church that gives us the sacraments, that gives us grace at every stage, and every day of our lives.

Mother, because it is our teacher.

The Church disposes us to pray and authorizes us to speak with God. It invites us to sing and fills us with the rapture of its liturgy even before we have gained any exact knowledge of it. It nourishes us with the mystery that is the presence of divine life.

It instructs and teaches us the substance of the two Testaments and initiates us into the Gospel, which it explains by infusing our minds with gifts of truth and wisdom and by training us to think of divine things. In fact it gives us what no teacher can give, and that is certainty. It guides us as children through our experience of the world, and as adults it is eager that we lead free and virtuous lives.

13. St. Cyprian, *Ep.*, 74, 7.
14. St. Augustine, *In Jo.*, 27.

Mother, because it loves us precisely as a mother does, that is to say more than anyone else.

It loves us as it makes of its authority a serving, and as it reminds those in command that they are pastors and obliged, if necessary, to give up their lives for the sake of their brothers.

It loves us by teaching the world that life is sacred, and by rebelling more than anyone else against any person who commits an outrage against the existence and dignity of a single human being.

It loves us, as it watches over every stage in our human condition: as children, it welcomes us, as youths exalts us, as adults blesses us, as elderly assists us, as we die comforts us, as deceased remembers us, as poor favors us, as sick heals us, as sinners calls us back, as penitents forgives us, and if we despair it gives us new life.

It loves us even when it seems to alienate itself from us. If we are haughty, wealthy and pleasure-loving it reprimands us, and if we are obstinate it punishes us while reminding us that we are pilgrims and hence must not tarry on our earthly journey.

And when the Church does become joined to us, it shows its love by discussing our problems and suggesting, as a wise friend might, ways of resolving them.

It loves us by giving us a fresh relish for thought in the form of its theology and mysticism, its action, goodness and holiness, its beauty and life, its inexhaustible art.

It loves us when it teaches us that we are brothers and that we must spread throughout the entire world this brotherhood, this wonderful Catholic unity that makes us one and good, original and universal, both in our work and in our peace.

It loves us, this holy mother, Christ's Church, because after all it holds a word, a grace, a promise for each one of us. And it awaits each one of us, invites each one of us . . .

And if we should in fact succeed in understanding the Church in a fresh way, and in acknowledging it as a mother who has been promoting and guarding our civilization for centuries, might we not display a greater confidence in it and dismiss as both ungrateful and unjust the resentment that has so frequently poisoned our relations with it?

And if we do acknowledge the Church to be a mother that covets neither temporal power nor social privileges but wishes to communicate its gifts of truth and grace, should we not feel ourselves inwardly its children, reborn in christian joy and christian hope?

Through the Mission that we all inaugurate tonight the Church our mother summons us, gently and firmly. And what shall we answer?

PART TWO

PART TWO

Ecumenical Councils in the Life of the Church

Incalculable Importance of the Ecumenical Council

The announcement of the forthcoming convocation of Vatican Council II has startled the Church and aroused the interest of the whole world. Few events have been heralded by such an interest. Everyone has the impression of being on the threshold of an extraordinary event, not only because it is something that so rarely occurs but also because of its incalculable importance in the course of history. Furthermore, we believers perceive darkly but intensely that this event is related to God's mysterious universal plan concerning our human destiny and is especially related to each one of us in our utter singularity of consciousness.

The evolution of civilization itself that runs its rapid course before our very eyes seems either to foreshadow a magnificent palingenesis or to threaten an apocalyptic catastrophe. It seems to furnish a view of the temporal world in the very act of awaiting a spiritual solution yet to be discovered. The messianism of our time that agitates and throbs under the great movements, whether optimistic or despairing, reacts with alarm as if it were synchronized with the unexpected announcement of the forthcoming Council. There is something prophetic in the air today, otherwise we would be unable to

129

explain why this announcement has aroused such intense attention and great expectation.

First of all, let us review what we are talking about. We are all familiar with the chronology of events. It is like the sudden sound of a bell ringing out in the dead of night, warning that time is running out and fulfilling destinies suddenly proclaimed between heaven and earth. On January 25, 1959, Pope John XXIII went to St. Paul's Basilica to celebrate the feast of the Apostle's conversion. Upon completion of the sacred rite and in the sole presence of the Cardinals assembled in that papal chapel, he announced, amidst general surprise, his intention of convening an ecumenical council in an allocution bearing these words: "Venerable Brethren and beloved sons! Trembling a little with emotion, but with humble firmness of purpose, we now tell you of a two-fold celebration: We propose to call a Diocesan Synod for Rome, and an Ecumenical Council for the Universal Church."[1]

We already know that the Pope has maintained his word with respect to the diocesan synod in Rome. And now we find ourselves present at the birth, out of those simple pontifical words, of the astonishing event that has been assuming enormous proportions in the Roman Curia and the Catholic Church, and at the same time confronts the whole world.

The surprise is justified, even for those who are somewhat experienced in the genesis of pontifical acts, rooted as they are in the administrative procedures of the departments and offices of the Roman Curia, and on occasion exclusively centered in the persons that surround the head of the Church. As far as we can learn this announcement, releasing as it does a decision of immeasurable importance, finds its origin in the Supreme Pontiff's sole and entirely personal will. He has received neither assistance nor advice from any quarter. Nobody has exerted any pressure or promised any results. Yet we are not faced with a despotic will, marked by a

1. *A.A.S.*, 1959, p. 58.

domineering and tyrannical psychology, but by a will that is naturally nurtured in a pastoral virtue that seeks out the good in and for others and fosters it with a spontaneous dedication.

Thus we are edified to discover what makes this act so certain and so successful: it stems from the Pope's human and fatherly heart. In summoning the Council the Pope was moved by an urgent transcendental need centered in his office as supreme pastor and teacher, the very vicar of Christ. Without having to suppose a preternatural charismatic impulse, we can certainly say—especially because of John XXIII's confidential revelations in this respect—that he was conscious of exercising, through the prophetic power of his office, the supreme power promised by Christ and guaranteed by the assistance of the Holy Spirit.

He himself informs us that he was obeying "an inspiration that he felt, in the humility of his heart, as a sudden and light touch." This first beginning, disclosed in the inner cenacle of the Pope's soul, is in itself very beautiful and very remarkable.

"This is something new in the history of the Church," writes Father Bevilacqua. "The council that Rome had feared for centuries because it had been turned into an anti-papal weapon by conciliarism is suddenly convened by the Pope without pressure and without the insistence of emperors, the clergy, or nations. The council that even four centuries ago was assembled more frequently by the will of a strong emperor than by that of a weak pope has come to pass today with joy and universal agreement through the simple invitation of a meek pope."[2]

We should mark well the singular form of the Council's origin so that we may modify, if this should indeed be necessary, the opinion that in any case is supported by wide experience: that great reforms, great acts of vitality within the

2. Rev. Bevilacqua in *Vita e Pensiero*, 1960, p. 513.

Church originate in the foundation, then rise to the summit whence they receive their definitions, their authority and their power to expand, and finally return to the foundation. Here on the contrary the act of renewal rises spontaneously and solely from the head and descends on the members. The Spirit watches from above.

The surprise is also justified for other reasons. The ecumenical council had indeed been discussed as one of several historical possibilities, but nobody had dared assign to this possibility any degree of predictable and concrete actualization. In fact, after the proclamation of papal infallibility at the end of the interrupted Vatican Council, some people doubted whether it would ever be possible to convene an ecumenical council again. Doellinger, the great adversary of this dogma, maintained that the recognized powers of Rome's bishop to rule and teach—powers which he believed had been granted in an undue and excessive degree—would absorb and annul the universal functions of the episcopal body.

The solemn dogmatic definition of the assumption of Mary most holy did in fact seem to confirm this doubt because Pius XII of venerated memory, before undertaking this act of his supreme teaching office, did wish to consult all the episcopate to find out whether the truth to be defined was a matter of the faith of the Church. But in point of fact he worked through correspondence, and by consulting individual bishops rather than the whole episcopal body assembled in collegial form. And so the prediction that the age of councils had definitively ended has been disappointed by the Pope's own spontaneous initiative, by his own deepened sense of an inner coherence with and a more sharply defined consciousness of his office as the Church's supreme head. The more the head recognizes himself as head, the more does he feel the need to join himself to the members and to celebrate together with them the mystery of the one organic life of the entire ecclesiastical body.

The Concept of Ecumenical Council

And so we are led to clarify briefly the concept of ecumenical council. The established concepts of canon law leave no doubt about the matter, and although the code provides no definition of an ecumenical council it does give us to understand that it is to be inferred chiefly from the composition of its members. We therefore learn that an ecumenical council is a solemn meeting of all the bishops in the world. The bishops participate in this meeting by divine right in so far as the episcopal body is successor to the apostolic college to which Christ has entrusted specific ecclesiastical powers.

By ecclesiastical law other ecclesiastics are associated with the bishops, and they are exactly specified: cardinals who are not bishops, heads of independent abbeys, abbots primate and abbots who are superiors of monastic congregations, and superiors general of exempt congregations of religious. One might argue about the extent of total participation that is required before the assembly can be said to be universal in character. This is in fact a recurring problem in the troubled history of the councils and one that canonists resolve by teaching that in order for a council to be genuinely ecumenical it is necessary that the prelates present be sufficient to be representative of the universal Church in response to a general and regular convocation.[3]

At this point we could raise many other subordinate questions: Are there any others that can by right participate in a council? Have not priests and even deacons also been present at some councils? And have not laymen themselves participated on occasion in conciliar meetings? Still more: since the Emperor Constantine convened the first ecumenical council, that of Nicea, and presided over it (if not officially then as

3. Wernz-Vidal, *De pers.*, pp. 452-453, in *Ius canonicum* (Romae, 1927-1946), 6 vols.

its protector and in an honorary position), do not civil authorities have a place, and do they not exercise authority in these great assemblies that after all do affect so many interests of civil life? In the history of the councils all these questions have received a vast, varied and vexed treatment, and have found a solution in the gradual elaboration of canon law culminating in the definitive solution given precisely in the code of canon law.[4]

The concept of ecumenical council is defined more exactly by means of two other elements, the one formal and the other finalistic. In order for there to be an ecumenical council the pope's authority is necessary as its informing, life-giving element. Since Peter has been made the head of the apostolic college and the episcopal body in turn succeeds the apostolic college, it follows that the episcopal body cannot subsist without Peter's successor, who is precisely the pope. St. Leo the Great gave a sharply chiselled definition of the Roman pontiff at the Council of Chalcedon where innumerable bishops had assembled: *per jussionem Leonis Romani Pontificis, qui est caput episcoporum.* The Roman pontiff is the head of the bishops.

This question has always been of the greatest interest and continues to occupy historians, canonists and theologians. This is the question that determines the pope's position in respect to the council and, in an even wider sense, the hierarchy's position in respect to the ecclesiastical community. And it is also the question that leads to a search for the source of the Church's authority, and that therefore completely affects the Church's own constitutional law.

For us the question has been resolved historically, dogmatically and juridically. It has been resolved historically

---

4. Canon 223. Cf. Karl Joseph von Hefele, *A History of the Councils of the Church* (Edinburgh: T. and T. Clark, 1871-1896), vol. I. (Page references are to the French edition, Paris, 1911, I, pp. 23ff; pp. 41ff.)

through the pope's authoritative intervention in validating those councils that we call ecumenical, that is to say that are binding on the whole Church and endowed, in regard to the definitions of the truths of faith, with the divine gift of infallibility.[5] It has been resolved dogmatically by the various definitions through which popes and councils have handed down decisions pertinent to this question.[6] Finally, it has been resolved juridically through the expressions, as simple as they are categorical, that have been recorded in canon law: "There can be no council unless it is convened by the Roman pontiff. It is the duty of the same Roman pontiff, in person or through his delegates, to preside over the ecumenical council, establish the matter to be treated and the order to be followed, as well as to transfer, suspend and dissolve the council itself, and confirm its decrees."[7]

This question has been resolved, as I was saying, and it is from its resolution that to a large extent the Catholic Church derives the clarity, solidity, balance, capacity to act and, I might say, that inner testimony, that consciousness of interpreting and actualizing Christ's thought which distinguishes its historical and spiritual life from that of the other christian denominations. In contrast, the question remains open in respect to these denominations that have been continuously tormented by a quest for the true ecclesiology.

The other element is finalistic. In order that there be a council rather than simply a conference or an institute or any sort of meeting whatsoever, the bishops' meeting with the pope must of necessity have as its object the exercising of the authority to teach and to govern that Christ has bestowed upon the apostolic college.

And now we should examine the reasons why councils are convened and why at the same time the sphere of their com-

5. Hefele, *op. cit.* pp. 41-79.
6. Cf. Denziger, *passim.*
7. Can. 222; cf. Petroncelli, *Elementi di Diritto Canonico,* n. 65.

petence is limited. The reasons for convening ecclesiastical synods may be manifold and of greater or lesser importance as the case may be, "but the chief purpose of all the councils," Hefele writes, "is without exception the search for the Church's welfare through a common resolution of all its pastors."[8]

Here, for example, are the words with which Pius IX convened the first Vatican Council: "When the Roman Pontiffs thought it would serve a useful purpose, chiefly in times of grave disorder and calamity for our holy religion and for civil society, they never hesitated to convene general councils for a variety of reasons: to hold discussions together with the bishops of the whole Catholic world who have been placed by the Holy Spirit to rule God's Church; to gather up its energies; to deliberate prudently and wisely about all that might contribute to defining the dogmas of faith; to denounce new errors and defend, illuminate, develop Catholic doctrine; to preserve and raise the level of ecclesiastical discipline and strengthen the lax morals of peoples."[9]

We could pursue further our analysis of the concept of the ecumenical council, but for the moment we need only view it in its solemn and extraordinary range. We shall say that it is an act of divine law,[10] so directly is it derived from the primordial authority that Christ bestowed upon the apostolic college. And so it is better to say that it is an act instituted by the Apostles and established under Christ's inspiration,[11] and therefore a collegial act of pastors placed at the head of the individual dioceses assembled around the Church's universal pastor. It is an act therefore that is responsive to the visible Church's unitarian, communitarian and organizing genius and that brings into relief the ecclesi-

---

8. Hefele, *op. cit.*, I, p. 9.
9. *Acta et Decreta Conc. Vat.*, VII, col. 2.
10. Wernz-Vidal, *op. cit.*, n. 457.
11. Hefele, *op. cit.*, I, p. 2.

astical government's monarchical, hierarchical and collegial constitution. It is an act of extraordinary jurisdiction in the face of pressing needs in the life of the Church and of society. It displays the greatest authority, that of the papacy—which in itself would suffice to regulate every question concerning the Church's rule. Yet in this case it invites the episcopal body to share in its authority. Even more, it unites its own authority with that of the episcopal body. In this fashion it brings out the universality of the ecclesiastical power, increases its inner capacity for supernatural life (Mt 18:20), and enlarges the possibility of a rapid and uniform propagation of the rules established by the councils.[12]

The Function of the Ecumenical Council

Yet despite all this the council is neither a permanent institution like a parliament, nor does it have a fixed schedule for meetings as the Council of Constance had intended with its famous decree *Sacrosancta* (1417). It is not a synthesis of the whole Church without distinction, as Gerson suggested in his equation *Ecclesia vel generale concilium*; nor does it transform the Church into a corporation represented and governed by a sovereign assembly to which the pope himself could be subjected. The council is one episode in the Church's life, a particular moment that does indeed affect the Church's supreme authority, yet does so not by creating that authority but simply by exercising it.

Its very singularity makes it extremely interesting and its function in the Church's life represents a supreme and extraordinary moment. Thus the question raised in this inaugural lecture is both warranted and spontaneous: what has been and continues to be the ecumenical council's function in the Church's life? However brief our answer, we are obliged to

12. Charles Journet, *The Church of the Word Incarnate* (London and New York: Sheed and Ward, 1955), Vol. I, pp. 397ff.

consider the ecumenical council under different aspects: juridical, theological, practical. But first of all, let us look at the historical aspect.

How many ecumenical councils have there been in the history of the Church? We know that some Catholic historians count nineteen ecumenical councils, some twenty, and that there are even some who count twenty-one. It depends on how the councils of Constance and Basle are interpreted, at least in reference to the respective recognition granted them by Martin V and Eugene IV.[13] Both Denziger, in the celebrated *Enchiridion Symbolorum,* and Wernz[14] include Constance alone, while other authorities exclude it.[15] We may therefore say that the forthcoming Vatican Council will be the twenty-first, that is, the twenty-first in the chronological series of ecumenical councils.

It is of interest to remember that the first eight ecumenical councils were celebrated in the East without the personal attendance of the popes. From the first centuries of the Church's life, even before the period of persecutions ended, councils of various sizes were assembled in different regions of the general area that christianity had reached. We all remember the fifteenth chapter of the Acts of the Apostles and how it relates that the first council, the Council of Jerusalem, was assembled in order to settle the controversy within the *Ecclesia ex gentibus.* It was in Jerusalem that the council manifested its transcendental source: ". . . it is the Holy Spirit's pleasure and ours . . ." (Acts 15:28), and in Jerusalem that it immediately asserted the universal vocation of the nascent Church.

"It was a solemn moment," Prat writes, "for it remained to be seen whether the christian society would vindicate the

13. Hefele, *op. cit.,* I, pp. 80ff.
14. Wernz-Vidal, *op. cit.,* pp. 444 and 446.
15. Cf. "Conciles," *Dictionnaire de Théologie Catholique,* pp. 670ff; *Initiation Théologique* I, pp. 196-197 (published in English as *Introduction to the Bible* by Fides).

universality the founder had promised it or whether it would persist in remaining a Jewish sect and hence, possibly, vanish into oblivion after a few years of sterile agitation. The retention of circumcision, with the integral observance of the Law that it entailed, would have meant renunciation of the hope of conquering the world. Never would the world become Jewish."[16] And so it was that the council was born in the Church.

Special synods followed, summoned to discuss problems both local and general in nature. Historians will recall the synods assembled against the Montanists in Asia Minor toward the middle of the second century, and those that were summoned to discuss the problem of dating the feast of Easter.[17]

At the moment, however, we are interested in surveying the conciliar phenomenon in its most general features. The eight ecumenical councils that were celebrated in the East can be classified succinctly as "dogmatic councils concerned about the fundamental doctrines of our religion": Nicea, on Christ's divinity (325); Constantinople I, on the Holy Spirit's divinity and consubstantiality (381); then Ephesus (431) and Chalcedon (451) on the one person and two natures of Christ. These are the first four councils to acquire unequalled authority in the ecclesiastical tradition. A century and a half later St. Gregory the Great, in announcing his election to the papacy to the Eastern patriarchs, does not hesitate to say that just as he accepts and venerates the four gospels so does he regard the four councils (Lib. I, *Eph.* 25).

The next two councils take place at Constantinople. The one is summoned by Justinian for the purpose of condemning the so-called three chapters, that is, the three bishops suspected of Nestorianism (553); the other is convened against Monotheletism for the purpose of affirming that Christ pos-

16. Cf. Pierre Battifol, *L'Église naissante et le catholicisme*, Paris, 1909, p. 73.
17. Eusebius, *Historiae ecclesiasticae*, Leipzig, 1908, V.

sesses two wills, the one human and the other divine (680). Nicene Council II condemns the Iconoclasts and Constantinople IV (870) deposes the Patriarch Photius.

At this point the division between the East and the West becomes deep-rooted and long lasting, though God does not wish it to continue indefinitely, especially in light of the fact that two other councils, those of Lyon (1274) and of Florence (1439-1445), did seek unsuccessfully to bring about a solid and true reconciliation. Anyone who wishes to explore the problem of the Eastern schism in the Church's life must begin with these councils that mark a complicated and continually sorrowful history that awaits its final resolution in the restoration of unity.

We should also speak of the other councils celebrated in the West; but others will do this in the course of this Congress. In our own synoptic survey of the ecumenical councils in the Church's life, however, we must stress the characteristic importance of two historical moments in which the activity of the councils played a crucial role in history: the period that included the councils of Constance and Basle in the fifteenth century and the period that included the Council of Trent in the sixteenth century.

It is well known that the councils of Constance and Basle follow upon a tragic period that involved a three-fold crisis which the inauspicious schism of the West engendered within the Church: a crisis of unity, of authority and of morals.[18] The conciliar assembly sought to overcome the crisis by attempting to arrogate to itself the Church's supreme power, to set itself up as a permanent institution and to transform the Church's government into a parliament at once arbitrary and exposed to all the influences of temporal events and interests. Nationalism became widespread in the Church and began to

---

18. Cf. Henry Daniel-Rops, *The Protestant Reformation,* translated by Audrey Butler (London: Dent; New York: Dutton, 1961); and his *The Catholic Reformation,* translated by John Warrington (London: Dent; New York: Dutton, 1962).

create a deep disunity that would be very difficult to overcome.

Yet the terrible ordeal was by no means fruitless because at bottom it succeeded in confirming the claim that unity and authority in Christ's Church must perforce coincide at the summit, that is to say, in the Roman pontificate.[19]

Next we turn to Trent, the longest ecumenical council, eighteen years in duration including interruptions: 1545-1563. Through its reforms this Council saved the Church's dogma and discipline, though it also marked that fatal separation of entire christian populations now known, sadly enough, by the name of Protestants. The new heresy, a contemporary historian writes, "may be summed up in two points: 1) the unilateral origin of faith, traced to Scripture exclusively; 2) the conception of the Church as purely spiritual and consequently subjectivistic, and a unilateral determination of the religious process: God is everything, man nothing. In answering these errors the Church proclaimed that 1) besides Scripture tradition is a legitimate source of faith and that it is the duty of the Church and of the Church alone to interpret the Bible; and that 2) the Church possesses a sacramental priesthood and seven sacraments that are authentic channels of grace. Moreover, the Church finds its center in the holy sacrifice of the Mass. Justification involves an inner transformation and not simply an outer coating . . ."

The Council of Trent's deepest significance does not lie in any one doctrine defined; neither does it lie in any one reform instituted: ". . . its importance consists chiefly in the fact that the Council was a true and proper concretization of the Catholic conception of the Church."[20]

More than three hundred years will pass before the convocation of a new ecumenical council, the Vatican Council.

19. H. Jedin, *A History of the Council of Trent,* translated by Dom Ernest Graf (London, New York: Thomas Nelson, 1957-61), 2 vols. (The page reference is to the Italian edition, Morcelliana, Brescia, 1949, v. I, p. 59.)
20. J. Lortz, *Storia della Chiesa nello sviluppo delle sue idee* (Alba, 1958), p. 312.

Opened on December 8, 1869, this council was interrupted by Pius IX. After Italian troops entered Rome, he issued the decree of October 20, 1870, whereby "after mature deliberation he suspended the celebration of the same ecumenical Vatican Council until a more suitable and opportune time."[21]

Though this council was unable to complete its agenda, it nevertheless marked a crucial moment in the Church's life as it reached a definition of the doctrine of papal infallibility in matters of faith and of the primacy of papal jurisdiction over all the bishops. In this respect the Vatican Council brings to an end an age-old process and opens up a new history in the exercise of papal power that is now firmly established and safeguarded. Yet, as eminent theologians were writing ten years ago, "unfortunately the problem of reconciling the episcopacy's divine rights with the divine rights of the pope has yet to be discussed, though a well balanced theology of the Church demands that this question be raised just as life requires that its practical implications be regulated. Will this work be the work of a second Vatican Council? This is a secret that lies hidden in the future."[22] Perhaps this secret will be disclosed during the long-awaited Vatican Council II, for which we are now preparing ourselves.

Another significant aspect of Vatican Council II must be noted: its consideration of a host of errors that arose in the last century and that constitute to a large extent the negative substratum of the modern mind. On two points especially the Vatican Council will take a position and nourish our contemporary Catholic thought with its statements on faith and reason. As it will clearly defend both,[23] it will furnish our culture with a fundamental defense for preserving and developing itself as both christian and human in character.

21. A. Saba, *Storia della Chiesa,* IV (Torino, 1945), p. 265.
22. "Vaticane," *Dictionnaire de Théologie Catholique,* 2583.
23. Cf. Denziger, 1806ff.

Expectations Surrounding the Forthcoming Ecumenical Council

So, as we stand at the threshold of the new ecumenical council we are naturally tempted to undertake to predict what it will do. It is of course difficult to say, though our great expectations are justified as the new Council may indeed assume spiritual and historical dimensions of incalculable importance. Our eagerness to know corresponds to the attitude, recommended by Christ, of knowing how to distinguish "the signs of appointed times" (Mt 16:4). Great things are stirring in the air and so we must be alert, we must try to understand God's designs, the movements of history, the currents of thought and the appointed time of responsibility.

Yet it remains difficult to say what the forthcoming ecumenical council will be like. Suffice it to say that we all harbor some fantasy in which we appear as reformers of the Church and that we all naturally dream that the proper moment has arrived for the fulfillment of our dreams. If the Council responds to God's designs, it is unlikely that it will fulfill our exact desires, no matter how competent we may believe ourselves to be. His design is ever so objective and transcendental, and certainly soars above our own countless subjective opinions. It is also enough to say that all the bishops and Catholic universities have already been invited to express their individual views in utter freedom. The Holy See is not short of sound advice, and the pope is not lacking in advance consultation concerning the Church's thought. The *sensus Ecclesiae* cannot receive a more ample or a freer expression.

And so the Church's consciousness of itself will furnish the great conciliar court with its subject matter, and the Church's lived and concrete experience will create the atmosphere in which it will speak. We may expect interesting reforms concerning the Church's internal government, its liturgy, its canon law, its ascetic life.

But if it is impossible to make concrete predictions, it does not seem impossible to anticipate a few general lines which the future Council may develop. In fact these general ideas are already present to some extent in certain premises that the ecumenical Vatican Council II would like to develop. First of all, will the new Council resume the topics that were interrupted by the suspension of Vatican Council I? Most likely, even if it should prefer to present itself as an autonomous, self-contained council rather than as a continuation of its predecessor.

The postulates of the first Council will undoubtedly be carried over into the second in respect to those problems that remained unresolved throughout the ninety years that have elapsed between the one and the other. The first Vatican Council longed for a definition of the assumption of Mary which, in the meantime, has been provided. A great many problems that were agitated at that time have been taken up again and treated in the ample and magnificent teaching of Leo XIII and succeeding popes. Thus the Code of Canon Law has resolved, in a practical way, more than a few of the debated questions, though others have remained unresolved. And we have already mentioned that it is desirable to complement the Church's doctrine concerning the episcopacy.

A scholar writes: "It does indeed seem that the forthcoming Council will especially insist on the Church's collegial character, for it is the Holy Father's considered thought to re-establish the value of this truth that is so deeply evangelical."[24]

A great many people are likewise hoping for a revision of the juridical relations between the religious congregations— that today still tend to be autonomistic and pluralistic—and the hierarchy, so that their specific functions, especially in the pastoral field, may be blended in a greater harmony.

24. Cf. Dom. Rousseau, quoted by A. Z. Serrand in *Signes du temps*, 8/9 (1960), p. 29.

In this fashion the Council's dogmatic and legislative decrees will probably throw some light on the layman's position in the Church. His active participation in its life will be understood as organically united to the discipline and spirituality of the hierarchy and the clergy.

Unlike many of the earlier councils, the forthcoming one meets in a peaceful and exciting moment in the Church's life. Without any more negative internal problems to resolve, the Church can now go about fostering internal gains. Neither heresies nor schisms nor dramatic difficulties within the Church summon the episcopacy to gather around the pope. There are other reasons that prompt the bishops to gather around the pope: a desire to enjoy their own inner unity, a duty to exercise their healthy vitality more efficiently, a need for sanctification and for an inner spiritual development. It is all of this that rallies the teaching Church together. It is for the sake of celebrating a moment of very rich and mystical spirituality that it meets, and it is for the sake of gaining a deeper consciousness of the mysterious correspondence between the Church's inner being—faith and charity—and its external, hierarchical and communitarian reality that the fateful hour draws near. And in that sublime moment it is absolutely certain that Jesus Christ the Lord, the Savior, the Teacher, the Son of God will be in the midst of his own who are gathered in his name.

A great German apologist and theologian of the last century, even though not always exact and complete, has nevertheless displayed a sublime vision in his celebrated work on the Church's unity that reads the past and prophesies the future. It was at the time when the Church's unity was most vigorously proclaimed, he says,

> that Christ's divinity was recognized in the most formal manner. That took place at the Council of Nicea, where for the first time all Christians were visibly assembled in the persons who represented their love.

It was then that they were able to recognize Christ in his full grandeur, for they themselves had become great. Oh! let us always be great and free; let us love incessantly and preserve unity intact in the bond of peace! For then it will be impossible for Christ's true greatness to escape us, because our eyes are pure and capable of contemplating him in all his purity.

I believe that if Moeller were alive today he would be filled with joy and hope over the announcement of the forthcoming Council that assembles in this very bond of peace.[25]

But will the Council serve only the internal purposes of the Catholic Church, or will the pastors of the world also look outside the paternal house to the actual world in which they live and which furnishes their apostolate with a most diversified, challenging and dramatic set of problems?

Undoubtedly the Council will also look beyond, for the Pope himself gives us cause to believe so. But how? we might ask. The Council will look in two directions. It will pray and it will speak: toward separated christians on the one hand, and toward contemporary life on the other.

The first problem, that of gathering our dissident brothers within the Church's unity, is very difficult and very complicated, and this is not the time to explain the reasons why. But this problem will certainly be examined at the forthcoming ecumenical council. Every effort will be made, indeed every sacrifice, to find some happy solution, though humanly speaking it is impossible to predict that the Council will succeed in decreeing a union less fragile than the union decreed by the councils of Lyon (1274) and Florence (1439-1445) in the case of the separated Eastern brothers.

Unfortunately, the history of separations is long and acrimonious, and the rifts that have been created seem today to be beyond repair. Even the ecumenical movement that we look upon with great reverence and immense interest may, in certain respects, delay and even obstruct rather than foster

25. Cf. Journet, *op. cit.*, p. 415.

an understanding with Rome. It will be very fortunate for Rome if its invitation to the separated churches should be spared the sad fate both of Pius IX's invitations on the eve of Vatican Council I and of the subsequent invitations that have been issued from time to time by the Apostolic See.

Great progress will be made if, at the forthcoming Council and under the auspices of Cardinal Bea who has been expressly assigned such a task, preliminary and friendly approaches can be made towards the dissidents. Great progress will likewise be made if we can establish those premises, involving a clear doctrine and reciprocal charity, that accentuate the need for reconciliation and at the same time obtain from Christ the grace necessary for bringing it about some day.

In any event, with the forthcoming Council the history of dissensions among christians opens up a fresh road towards peace and unity, for today that history records neither polemics nor excommunications nor wars but rather a programmatic intention of achieving a reconciliation. Let us listen to this intention as it is revealed in the moving words of John XXIII's first encyclical, *Ad Petri Cathedram*. Addressing separated christians, this is what he says: "May we, in fond anticipation, address you as sons and brethren? May we hope with a father's love for your return? . . . When we fondly call you to the unity of the Church, please observe that we are not inviting you to a strange home, but to your own, to the abode of your forefathers . . . 'I am . . . Joseph, your brother' (Gn 45:4). 'Come, make room for us' (2 Cor 7:2) We want nothing else but your salvation, your eternal happiness. Come! This long-desired unity, fostered and fed by brotherly love, will beget a great peace."[26]

A great hope has been kindled in the Church, and blessed is he who has given us its joyful light.

26. *A.A.S.*, 1959, pp. 515 and 517. Also in *The Pope Speaks*, vol. 5, No. 4 (Autumn 1959), 400.

Then the forthcoming ecumenical council will undoubtedly look in the other direction, towards contemporary life. And what will it see? Will it see an incredibly swift transformation of our way of life, that requires the attention and adaptation of pastors? Will it see the secular, materialistic, marxist humanism that makes a reaffirmation of a religious and christian humanism imperative? Or the anti-intellectual decomposition and moral disintegration of our age that already distinguish it for its cries of anguish and for its silent, cynical despair? Will it see a world resplendent with technical and scientific progress, yet darkened by frightful shadows that snuff out God's light? Or a humanity that spurns the need for salvation and goes about creating the fatal premises and catastrophic instruments for its own destruction?

Here too it is difficult to say, though it does seem certain that a powerful effort will be made for a dialogue. And if not for a dialogue, then for a lament, a call, a prophecy. It will be necessary to oppose the glory of christian truth and charity to the enlightened but rationalistic rule of terrestrial hopes, and the rule of God and love to the rule of atheism and egotism. Finally, a highly civilized and advanced world is engaged in search, marked by suffering, but journeying unwittingly towards Christ. Pastors must not change the direction of these hard won and hospitable paths, the paths of human dignity, brotherhood, unity and peace. On the contrary, they must say in an unmistakable tone capable of causing the human heart to leap: turn and look, for there is Christ.

Let Us Think About the Council

Importance of the Event

Venerable brothers and beloved children!

1. We are writing this pastoral letter in Rome where we have been summoned for the preparatory meetings of the Ecumenical Council that will open this year, 1962, as the Holy Father our Pope John XXIII has solemnly announced in the bull *Humanae Salutis* of December 25, 1961. In fact the Pope's announcement has informed us that Vatican Council II will open on October 11.

The importance of this event is so great that this year we cannot choose any other theme for our principal annual instruction, even though the grand and unique character of the announced Ecumenical Council has already provoked a thousand explanations, comments and good wishes, and the preparations for it filled the world with news and expectations: *in omnem terram exivit sonus eorum,* "their utterance fills every land . . ." (Ps 18:5).

2. We too have spoken a great deal about the Council. From the very moment that the Pope first made his announcement, we ourselves have cried out in wonder, joy and hope, and have exhorted you "immediately to understand God's time."[1]

1. *Rivista Diocesana milanese,* p. 73 and pp. 101-102.

149

Publications, lectures, congresses, instructions, prayers have already spread information and aroused sentiments that would seem to suffice for opening up our hearts to the forthcoming celebration of the Council. Yet we do not believe it useless to invite you, through this our Easter message, to a fresh meditation on a theme of such breadth and weight: first of all, we must reorganize our ideas about the Ecumenical Council; next, we should gain a deeper understanding not only of its historical and external meaning but also of its inner, spiritual, human and religious significance. At the same time we should immediately experience the mysterious and as it were intoxicating richness of this singular event. It is not only men living in this world who are its protagonists. It is also—and even more so—the Holy Spirit, who breathes life into Christ's Church and who will soon speak in that setting, at that time. We should therefore review our own thoughts about the Council, arrange them more systematically and prove their validity as far as possible. This we should do especially since we have aroused a few ideas, some sound, some fanciful, in everybody—and particularly in more religious and zealous souls. The Council poses a vast number of extremely interesting topics in respect both to the Church's inner life and its impact on the world's spiritual and moral life. We must order these topics somewhat in our minds so that we may grasp their meaning and importance more thoroughly. We shall see how to do this shortly. Finally, we must convince ourselves more firmly that this event is universal in character. For the Council concerns us too, not only because in some way it touches our own interests and destinies but also because we must all participate in it, to a certain extent, if we really claim to be faithful members of Christ's mystical body. It is the whole Church that expresses itself in the Council, and we are the Church.

It is necessary in the meantime that all of us, as single persons and as communities, should prepare ourselves for the Council, participate in it as far as possible, and then open ourselves to it in response, for without this communion of mind and purpose the Council will never attain its ends completely.

3. This vision of the extraordinary importance of the forthcoming Ecumenical Council becomes wider and clearer to us at the present moment here in Rome, where we have spent the greater part of our life. While we were humbly yet diligently at work in the offices of the Apostolic See, we always made every effort to penetrate the Church's mystery, to discover and to some extent arouse, under the guidance of Peter's succesor, the signs that mark the perennial vitality of christianity.

And once again we are surprised at the deep emotion and many thoughts that Rome invariably arouses in us. We are so overcome that we feel compelled to confide in you a little, almost as a preface to the instruction that we are about to present on the eve of the Council, thoughts that here in Rome seem to find their most authentic and widest audience.

Why Is the Council in Rome?

4. In fact, the concept of Rome, it seems to us, should be linked intelligently with the concept of the Council. We do not believe this simply because an ecumenical council takes place solely in Rome, for in point of fact most of the councils did not meet here. On the other hand, it is evident that an ecumenical council does find its most suitable location in Rome, and its location does undoubtedly accentuate the prominence of a given event, just as an event enlivens a place with its own inner light. Rome is the city of unity, the city of authority, of truth, of charity. Rome is the center of the Catholic world, the city of universality.

And what is an ecumenical council if not the celebration of these human ideals that only Christ's religion actualizes, sanctifies and gives eternal vitality? Rome is the Church's city, and a council is a moment in the Church's plenitude. Rome is Christ's city, and a council is a moment in Christ's mystical and operative presence in his Church and in the world.

5. Thus it seems to us that the Council will furnish Rome a sublime moment, one perhaps of unsurpassed splendor, and will infuse it with an incomparable vigor so that it may proclaim God's words to men and men's words to God. A charismatic grace of prophecy will animate the City; the human city will be transformed into the city of God. Rome will become Jerusalem.

6. Two thoughts chiefly have sprung up in our mind in the midst of these agitated sentiments and ideas that Catholic Rome usually arouses in those who contemplate it—two thoughts which, like the others we have mentioned, are confirmed by countless witnesses, so easy is it to experience them in this blessed atmosphere. One is the thought of *Roma patria communis*: nobody is a stranger in Rome, if he but gives himself to its peculiar genius. All who will converge on Rome for this solemn meeting will be neither strangers nor guests nor travellers: they will be citizens. Those who make a pilgrimage to Rome know and in a mysterious way experience that they have become citizens of the true mankind. This feeling will be even more intense in those who will soon come to Rome to carry out an office—the Church's magisterium—that is universal in nature: they will feel at home. For it is wonderful that there should be a place in the world and in history where everybody can feel himself at home. Even secular men, even non-believers, experience this mysterious feeling in Rome.[2]

2. We read, for example: "I had a marvellous feeling of being at home, a feeling that remained with me until the very moment that I left. I do not believe it can be completely explained by the fact that from early youth we have become familiar with a great many monuments through the reproductions that we have

And that the Council should assume this sense of community, of brotherhood, of family, for the sole reason that it is convened in Rome, seems to prepare us to understand its meaning better and to appreciate its value more.

7. Our second thought is of the hope that always seems to be in the air in Rome, though it is not always noticed, and that is the hope that seems to be engaged in a search for its own home. This hope has something messianic, something eschatological about it. It is not correct to define Rome only as an ancient city that has survived in the form of a modern capital.[3] Rome possesses a destiny that looks ahead into the future. Its history is not over, nor is the present sufficient to actualize the potentiality of its mission in time.

There is an expectation in Rome, a logic that must be developed to reach a fresh aim. These are the premises in Rome that we must be sure to retain as promises. In Rome nothing has ended; everything has just begun. Human needs find their supreme court of appeal in Rome, and in Rome faith and the art of human perfectibility are at home as in their castle and work-shop. On Roman soil pessimism is out of place. Here in Rome we find that redemption is always possible, that peace is always attainable, and that human progress can always be pursued. Here it is that true humanism is perennially cultivated.

In so far as the familiar biblical words, "Let us make man" (Gn 1:26) in the likeness of God (that is, according to the

---

seen. I should prefer to think that Rome is innate in every human being, that it is like an ideal native land to which we cling with something that is within us, from which all of us have derived some benefit. No matter how great or wretched we may be, we may say that Rome reveals to us, with inexorable truth, what truly dwells within us . . ." S. Negro, *Seconda Roma,* ix-x.

3. Cf. Ferdinand Gregorovius, *History of the City of Rome in the Middle Ages,* translated by Annie Hamilton (London: G. Bell and Sons, 1894-1912), 8 volumes. (Page references are to the Italian edition: I, pp. 5-6).

most sublime model) make us dissatisfied with our achievements, they constitute a program. For here Christ is in process: ". . . until I can see Christ's image formed in you!" (Gal
4:19). This is the burden, this the mission of Catholic Rome:
to preach and communicate Christ with an impassive indifference to difficulties and persecutions, and with an unshaken
trust in his glorious final return. And the fact that the Council—that is, the whole Church as it is engaged in preaching
and evangelizing—should convene in Rome shows that its
hopes, unfurled like a flag, are caught up in history; they
spread throughout an uneasy and unsettled world as a beacon
that guides and comforts.

8. Hence the Ecumenical Council provides a great theme
and could occasion a varied and lengthy discourse. For the
purposes of our simple pastoral letter it is enough to recall
that the theme is so profound, complex and sacred that none
of us will be too prompt to pronounce a hasty and superficial
judgment. It will also be enough to mention a few of its
aspects in order to gain some precise concepts. These in turn
should help us, in our devotion, to participate spiritually in
the great event, and to discover and meditate on those aspects
of the Council that we believe will edify us as faithful members of the Church, and educate us as children of our own
century.

The Expectation of the Entire Christian Community

9. The Council reveals its most obvious aspect in the very
fact of its convocation. Without the slightest suspicion on
anybody's part, the Council is convened by the Holy Pontiff's
sole and free will. The announcement was enough to make
the whole Church, and the whole world, feel that an extraordinary event was about to take place. It was exactly as if
it had been expected. The event immediately took on the

aspect and force of a truly universal call. It was like the ground-swell of a reawakened vitality pervading the whole Church.

The Pope would be in touch with all the bishops, beyond the ecclesiastical circle of the Roman Curia, so that he might reach the vast range of the universal hierarchy. We could say that if the external chain of events that we call history had not awaited this event, the Catholic spirit did. In fact, though perhaps not consciously, the Catholic world brought these events to a head. And it is precisely this call, let us add, that it needed.

Though it has suffered greatly in recent years, the Catholic spirit has never failed to display a remarkable vitality. It has been subject in our generation to the richest, strangest and most dramatic experiences. It has been tried by the suffering and consequences of wars, tormented in many countries by crude oppressions and persecutions, corroded by crises of thought and morals engendered by modern evolution, and attacked by the most radical forms of secularism and atheism. Yet despite all this it has been alive and aflame with fresh energies in every particle of its being: in its thought, faith and sanctity, in the celebration of its liturgical mystery, in its pastoral care, its missions and its organizational growth, in its works of charity, in its encouragement of the laity to broaden the community of the church, in the spreading of christian principles in the manifold fields of temporal society —in all this the Catholic spirit, in joy and veneration, has heard Rome speak. All this while it was receiving rules and instructions which it obeyed willingly, though it frequently believed that it lacked the facilities for a dialogue, that it had not been invited to collaborate, that the Church's unity had to be lived in passive acceptance rather than celebrated in the fraternity fostered by that very unity itself. In so many sectors of its world-wide existence the Catholic spirit felt an exhilarating experience, a desire to confide in and petition Rome, and to relate itself, by means of a more lively language, not only to Rome but to its own exigencies.

And so when the Pope announced the Ecumenical Council it seems that he had divined a hidden expectation not only on the part of the Episcopal College but of the entire Catholic world as well. A flame of enthusiasm swept over the whole Church. He understood immediately, perhaps through inspiration, that by convening the Council he would release unequalled vital forces in the Church.

Never had the Catholic Church been taken by surprise as it was by this call, and never had it been in such a state of good will and in such need of communing with Christ's vicar and his brothers scattered throughout the world. This first aspect of the Council constitutes by itself an historical event of the greatest importance and spiritual value for the whole Catholic world. It is a call for a great dialogue concerning the Church's inner unity.

10. How does this dialogue take place?

A fact of such proportion and complexity must be treated with the utmost rigor. This is the Council's second aspect, the juridical and ecclesiastical element, and it too is open for everyone to see. We shall not dwell at length on this external and, so to speak, concrete and material side of the Council. But we shall draw some ideas from the Church's law. In language that is now current, a Council is, in itself, an assembly of bishops. When the pope convenes all the bishops in the world a council is called ecumenical, that is, universal; it could also be called, properly speaking, catholic.

It is no ordinary assembly, as if it were a social meeting of friends or a study group or a prayer meeting. On the contrary, it is an assembly of the Church's governing body: that is, one that deliberates about matters of doctrine and discipline. And in a council the Church's magisterium and jurisdiction find their clearest and most solemn expression.

Religious questions therefore (that is, those that have to do

with the Church's faith, morals and discipline) are the proper
topic for a council, and its objective is the spiritual and moral
welfare of the christian people, and indirectly of the whole
world.

11. We may advance a descriptive and purely juridical
definition of an ecumenical council in the following terms:
it is a solemn assembly of the bishops of the whole world,
which the Roman pontiff convenes for the purpose of delib-
erating together, under his authority and presidency, about
religious problems that concern the whole of christendom.[4]

The council therefore is the supreme form of the Church's
magisterium and government.

The Primacy of Peter, the Church's Foundation

12. It is extremely important for us to understand the pope's
position in respect to an ecumenical council. We must remember that by himself alone the pope possesses supreme and
plenary power of jurisdiction over the entire Church. This
power, ordinary and proper, is "episcopal," that is to say
pastoral, and comes immediately from Christ and not from
the Church. When he speaks solemnly (*ex cathedra*) he
enjoys a special divine assistance that has been promised
through the person of Peter the Apostle and that makes his
definitions infallible. Consequently they are irreformable by
virtue of his own power, and not by the consent either of other
bishops or of the Church.[5] This has been defined by Vatican
Council I, interpreting Christ's thought and the Church's age-
old faith.[6] The pope's power is "vicarious" in respect to

---

4. "Conciles," *Dictionnaire de Théologie Catholique,* col. 641.
5. Cf. Denz. 1839; cf. St. Gregory the Great, who writes to the
   bishops assembled in Constantinople in 599: "Let them consider
   nothing whatsoever without the authority and approval of the
   Apostolic See," *P.L.* 77, col. 1005.
6. "The papacy does not derive its origin and power from the
   Church. When Jesus Christ, true God, willed to create the
   papacy and the pope, he had recourse neither to the Church's

Christ, but in respect to the Church it is proper, supreme and universal.

13. Therefore the pope can act with full authority and efficacy without a council, although even when he does exercise this authority he never acts without being conscious of the fact that he is in communion with the bishops and the Church. Nevertheless it is he and he alone who confirms the faith of all, and without him a council can have no validity.

Of necessity it is the pope who must convene and preside over a council, or at least ratify its deliberations. While a council adds no substantial validity to the pope's authority, it is absolutely essential that it be united with the pope in order that it have its specific efficacy. Rather than distinguishing its own jurisdiction from that of the pope, a council identifies itself with it and constitutes, together with him, the supreme power in the whole Church.[7] Clearly then a council is not indispensable to the Church's government, though when it gathers around the pope the Church's government does assume its most solemn form, most evident in its plenitude and consequently eminently efficacious.

Christ has set Peter's primacy at the head of his Church as necessary and sufficient for governing it; but he has also instituted the apostolic college and endowed it, in communion with Peter, with the power and the mandate of the magisterium and the care of souls.

---

nor the Apostles' ministry, but did so by saying directly to Peter: feed my flock." *Summa Theologiae*, II, II, I, 10, 3. Cf. Journet, *The Church of the Word Incarnate*, I, p. 422: "We conclude: 1) that the Pope is the Vicar of Christ, not of the Church; 2) that he holds his authority directly from God, the Church's election merely going to designate a successor for Peter; 3) that of all existing governments the papacy is the sole government by divine right, the only one which is sovereign in the strict sense."

7. Can. 228, S I. Cf. Veillet, *Les États généraux de l'Église*, (Paris: Fleurus, 1961).

A council comes into existence the moment this communion of government becomes fully manifest. The primacy of power that Peter holds and transmits to the bishop of Rome becomes fused with the Apostles' collegial power that is transmitted to the episcopacy. And let us not forget that Peter was the first but not the only apostle. A council therefore is not only a special and solemn occasion in the Church's government; it is the moment that shows forth fully the mystery of the teaching Church as well as the mystery of its distinctive notes: apostolicity, unity, catholicity and holiness.

14. Consequently, since Vatican Council I has defined the plenitude of papal power it is no longer possible to believe the totally unfounded claim that councils are superfluous. We believe the opposite, and our belief is already borne out by the convocation of the forthcoming Council. There could still have been some hesitation about this convocation of the Council—it might have been plausible—had there still been some doubt about a council's authority in respect to the pope (as did in fact happen at the councils of Constance and Basle). But since this constitutional truth about papal supremacy in respect to a council has already been defined in the Church, the chief obstacle to holding an ecumenical council has vanished. Thus, no longer suspect because of possible internal dissension, ecumenical councils can become a magnificent source of spiritual energies for the whole Church.

15. In a council the Church's mystery, we were saying, shines forth as never before. Pius IX had already taught this: "It is in the ecumenical council that the holy dogmas of religion are defined most deeply and expressed most amply, that ecclesiastical discipline is restored and most solidly established . . . that the bond between the Church's members and its head is strengthened, that the vigor of Christ's whole mystical body is increased. . . ."[8]

16. And the pope's supreme authority does not thereby

8. Cf. "Const. Die Filius," *Coll. Lac.* VII, 248.

annul the bishops' authority, as some Catholics have suspected[9] and as many of our separated brothers still assert.[10]
Though bishops do receive their full priestly powers from the
sacrament of orders, it is the supreme pontiff who vests them
with jurisdiction over their respective dioceses.

Rather than reducing the bishops' authority, the pope's
authority sustains it, and in fact finds its own honor in the
dignity and stability of that authority. Pope Gregory the
Great had already asserted this when he wrote to the bishop
of Alexandria: "My honor is one with the universal Church's
honor. My honor is one with my brother's strength and pros-
perity. It is only when the honor that is due to each one of

9. Dejaifve, S. J., *Pape et Evêques au premier Concile du Vatican*
(Paris: Desclée de Brouwer, 1961).
10. Concerning the problem connected with the relations between
episcopacy and the pontifical primacy, see the article by Monsignor Carlo Colombo, "Episcopacy and Pontifical Primacy in
the Church's Life," in *Scuola Cattolica*, Nov.-Dec., 1960, 401-
434. The encyclical "Mystici Corporis" (*A.A.S.*, 1942, 212)
has clarified the doctrine concerning the derivation of episcopal
jurisdiction from the pontifical power. Colombo writes (*ibid.*,
p. 421): "In so far as they constitute a legitimate part of the
episcopal college and remain in communion with it, the bishops
participate in the Church's apostolic powers and in fact receive
their own 'powers' from Jesus Christ through the episcopal college. The episcopal power is not acephalous. On the contrary,
it does have a head that even by itself possesses the plenary
'apostolic powers' that are necesary for the life of the Church
as a whole. And it is precisely this complexus of powers that
contains, as in its source or root, every power of every single
bishop. This it seems to me, is how we can and should explain
the origin of that jurisdictional power that the bishops hold
from the Roman pontiff, as the encyclical "Mystici Corporis"
teaches us. It must not be understood as an uninterrupted transmission of jurisdiction that historically has not existed for long
centuries. It is a power that must rather be understood as a
radical derivation of the particular from the general power that,
according to Catholic teaching, already exists in a plenary way
in the Roman pontiff alone even without the Council's cooperation. The actual transmission of jurisdiction is now a common
historical fact . . ."

my brothers is not refused to them that I myself am truly
honored."[11]

17. Other questions need to be answered, and will in fact
find their answer in the impact created by the event itself.
There are such questions as the frequency of councils; whether
the meetings should be fixed or flexible or irregular; and on
whom and what they should depend. Can other less solemn
councils exist, special in character (on appeal from the pope
to the council—by now undoubtedly illegitimate)? What
will be the method of voting at the council? There are many
questions of this sort.

18. One question in particular should be stressed, the
question concerning the persons who are today to be convened, according to canon law. From the bull cited above we
learn that the following ecclesiastics will be summoned to the
forthcoming Council: cardinals, patriarchs, primates, arch-
bishops, bishops and auxiliary bishops, heads of independent
abbeys, abbots and prelates with jurisdiction, abbots primate,
abbots who are superiors of monastic congregations, and
superiors general of exempt congregations of religious.

19. A council therefore is neither a parliament elected by
the people nor is it an assembly of experts, professors, theologians and canonists; it is rather an organ composed of ecclesiastics who are invested with their own authority and an
assembly of pastors and doctors of Christ's Church. These
doctors and pastors do not hold their specific office through
any personal title or claim of either noble or dynastic succession, nor again through any local historical privilege. They
hold their office because they have been legitimately called
to succeed the apostles, if they are bishops, and because they
have been invested with a power and dignity that presuppose
a call from above, and that may fall upon the shoulders of
any person whatsoever who is deemed suitable for that sublime and solemn office, without distinction of class, nation or

11. Cf. Charles Journet, *op. cit.*, I, pp. 382ff.

race. Though authority in the Church does come from above
—that is, springs solely from Christ and not from the community—it does not fear to descend below and choose its
own with the greatest possible freedom. Such is the Church.
We should reflect on this aspect of a council's composition
too, so that we may admire God's work in a spectacular
human phenomenon.

20. If then at a council's sessions only those sit who are
entrusted with carrying out "the service of authority" in God's
Church, it is clear why the other members of the community
of believers, priests, religious and laymen, are not present.
Yet the whole community is present in a council because it
is there that its faith is expressed and its interests are treated;
it is there that the pastors who guide, interpret and represent
it are assembled.

If a council were conceived as a meeting of ecclesiastics
separated from the rest of the Church, its character as the
synthesis of the Church would be unintelligible. The priesthood is for the faithful, and where a given assembly's sacerdotal composition is most pronounced, there the moral presence of the christian people is most marked. Thus the whole
Church will be present in a council because without it neither
the pope nor the bishops are conceivable.

21. Today no civil authorities will be present at the meetings of the Council. At one time they did attend and did discharge various functions, though none of these functions were
intrinsically relevant to the exercise of the Church's magisterium. But today, in the light of the progressively more exact
distinctions that modern public law has drawn between civil
and ecclesiastical society, the intervention of civil authorities
in the Council is neither possible nor desirable. The Church
appears there alone, defenceless yet free in its most complete
and fundamental manifestation.[12]

22. These remarks should prompt us to look at the history

12. Cf. Hefele, *op. cit.,* I, 41, n. 3, 47-48, 52, 57, etc.

of the councils, but we would thereby be distracted from our object, which is not so much to inform as to suggest the religious significance of the council for which we are preparing. From the history of the ecumenical councils we will make only one observation, and that concerns the episcopacy's collegial character in so far as it is successor to the apostolic college.

Just as Peter is the head of the apostolic college so the pope is the head of the episcopal college. And here we stand at the very center of the Church's constitutional law. Therefore the assembly of the episcopal college through the pope's mediation takes place by divine law.[13]

Christ is the mainspring of the ecumenical councils.

23. And then the long sequence of these great assemblies[14] will show us the ages-long journey of ecclesiastical history,

13. Wernz-Vidal, *Jus canonicum*, II, p. 444, n. 457. Christ has not determined the obligation nor set the time or specified the method for conducting a council. All this he made subordinate to the power of the keys, that is, to the plenary jurisdiction over the whole Church that he gave to Peter.

14. Twenty-two ecumenical councils are usually recognized by including both the Council of Jerusalem, recounted in the Acts of the Apostles (ch. 15, 6-29), and the forthcoming Vatican Council. The dissident Eastern Church recognizes only the first eight ecumenical councils (some within it recognize just seven), all of them celebrated in the East and convened by the emperors with the approval of the popes (cf. Duchesne, *Églises séparées*, 1896, quoted by Journet, *op. cit.*, p. 420). After the Council of Constantinople IV (868-870) there is a break until 1123 when Pope Calixtus II convened Lateran Council I. Since that time all the ecumenical councils have taken place in the West. As there has been some dispute over the ecumenical character of the Council of Basle (1431), later continued in the Council of Ferrara-Florence (1438-1442), there is no universal agreement about the total number of ecumenical councils (cf. Hefele, *op. cit.*, I, p. 79ff). "The recognition of the ecumenical character of the twenty assemblies cannot be traced back to one comprehensive legislative act of the popes. Their ecumenical character was only established by the theological schools as a whole and by actual practice" (H. Jedin, *Ecumenical Councils of the*

and point to the most dramatic and decisive moments of christianity in the world: moments in which it was important to define the meaning of God's revealed word, vindicate the Church's freedom, reconstitute its unity and release its inmost and real vitality from its very center.[15]

The Divine Mystery of the Church, Christ's Mystical Body

24. And here we are obliged to look more deeply into this recurrent historical phenomenon. It has played a very large role in the Church's life, determining its thought and spirituality, renewing the vigor of its compact internal structure and ensuring its longevity. The Church is not a mere institution that is visible and composed of men. It is not simply an extraordinary historical phenomenon. It is a body of doctrines, precepts and rites. The Church is a mystery:[16] that is, a divine design, a divine presence, a divine action.

Design, presence, action, mysteriously visible and mysteriously hidden. Those men will see, and understand, and rejoice who have the grace of faith and a lucidity of mind joined with a will that is loving and ready to accept and live the faith. This inner and mysterious vision of the Church

---

Catholic Church: an Historical Outline [New York: Herder and Herder, 1960], pp. 3-4). It is also common knowledge that throughout its history the Church has convened innumerable non-ecumenical councils: general, national, provincial, diocesan.

15. Cf. N. Mosconi, *Vigilia Conciliare* (Rovigo, 1961); and various authors in *Le Concile et les Conciles* (Paris: Ed. du Cerf, 1960).

16. Cf. Henri De Lubac, *The Splendour of the Church,* translated by Michael Mason (New York: Sheed and Ward, 1956); J. M. Congar, *The Mystery of the Church: Studies,* translated by A. V. Littledale (Baltimore: Helicon, 1960); H. Clerissac, O. P., *Le Mystère de l'Église* (1918); Hasserveldt, *Il Mistero della Chiesa* (Rome: Ed. Paoline, 1956); Romano Guardini, *The Church and the Catholic and The Spirit of the Liturgy,* translated by Ada Lane (New York: Sheed and Ward, 1935).

will be made easier for us to perceive if we first look at its external and historical form, for in virtue of its unmistakable notes, it bears the sign of its own truth.[17]

25. The Church is a mystery that must be sought in God's mind. We must learn how to make this effort to search for the Church's origin in God's thought humbly, attentively and lovingly, by making use of Holy Scripture. When we undertake this search we shall immediately find ourselves faced with a sublime discovery: even before we set out in search of God, God had already sought us! "He gave us his love first" (1 Jn 4:10, 19). And the Church (that is, humanity united in Christ) is nothing but the fulfillment of God's plan to love us. It is God who seeks his people and builds his Jerusalem in the Old Testament (Eccl 24:11ff.), and it is God who, in the New Testament, shapes his people according to the image of his Son whom he sends, out of love, to redeem the world (Rom 8:29; Jn 3:16).

26. In fact, the Church is Christ's continuation in time and his extension on earth: it is his living presence. With the Church's authority and teaching, "He who listens to you, listens to me" (Lk 10:16). In the Church's legitimately constituted community, "Where two or three are gathered together in my name, I am there in the midst of them (Mt 18:20). In the ever-present activity of the apostolic succession, it is always Christ who speaks: "And behold I am with you all through the days that are coming, until the consummation of the world" (Mt 28:20). And the mystery of the eucharistic sacrifice will perpetuate Jesus' ineffable presence among us: "So it is the Lord's death that you are heralding whenever you eat this bread and drink this cup until he comes" (1 Cor 11:26).

27. The Church is his salvific action, that is, the means and vehicle for this salvific action; it is the instrument for

17. Journet, op. cit., pp. 526ff. Cf. Newman, Apologia pro vita sua, passim.

exercising the power of orders in administering the sacraments, and a subordinate coadjutor in exercising the power
of jurisdiction, a free and human secondary cause.[18] The
Holy Spirit, sent by Christ as the Church's life-giving force,
engenders grace in the Church through his charisms and
gifts.[19]

28. The meeting of an ecumenical council calls all this to
our attention and makes it, at it were, evident. That Christ
assists his Church becomes evident in the very fact that this
event is being actualized in complete agreement with his
original word.

This is the thought that is woven in the bull by which Pope
John XXIII announces the Council: "Before Jesus Christ,
who had re-opened the way to salvation for mankind, as-
cended into heaven, he gave the Apostles he had chosen a
command to carry the light of the Gospel to all nations, and
he willingly made a promise to them that would confer authority and stability upon the office he had committed to
them: 'Behold I am with you all days, even to the consummation of the world.' There has never been a time when this
constant, joyful presence of Christ has failed to show itself
alive and at work in the holy Church, but it has shone forth
most clearly at times when mankind and society were being
buffeted by unusually fierce storms."[20]

As we were saying (cf. no. 13), here the Church's notes
shine forth, for here in the Council, as never before, it manifests itself one, holy, Catholic and apostolic. As never before
the Church's divine-human consciousness proclaims: "It is
the Holy Spirit's pleasure and ours that . . ." (Acts 15:18).
So we hear the Apostles pronounce at the first Council of
Jerusalem and so the fathers of Vatican Council II will speak.

18. Journet, *ibid.*, I, 50ff.
19. Cf. St. John's narrative of the Last Supper, especially chapters
    14 and 16.
20. Cf. The Bull *Humanae Salutis*, December 25, 1961; toward the
    beginning. Also in *The Pope Speaks*, vol. 7, no. 4, 353.

29. Thus we are strengthened by the certitude that God loves, Christ assists, and the Holy Spirit guides the Church. On the threshold of experiencing this somewhat ourselves, we must look at the Council with great reverence and great hope. And we must be ready to discern in the intentions that move the Pope to convene this ecumenical council signs, as it were, of the divine will.

What does our Lord want from this Council?

To understand God's will would be a great achievement indeed, for then the mysterious and loving work of providence would, to some extent, be revealed to us as it enters into a dialogue with history (that is, the sum total of free human wills) and prepares fresh destinies for individual people, and the whole world. And immense vistas would thus be opened up to us: of graces pouring down from heaven, of responsibilities summoning us to make crucial choices, of fresh energies springing from the depths of human hearts, of wondrous combinations of ages and events, of threads running from the closely-knit woof of yesterday and today towards the morrow, towards the future—and, beyond time, towards the final event of Christ . . .

Christians are not altogether blind to this stupendous, if still forever dimly luminous vision. But in order that we may gaze upon this glowing penumbra, it is necessary as I say to fix our mind on the Pope's intentions. We must remember that in this case too he is a mediator, reflected and visible to us, of the one sole invisible mediator, Christ the Lord; a mediator, that is, between the things of heaven and the things of earth.

What are the Pope's intentions concerning the forthcoming ecumenical council?

30. Before repeating the well known answer to this question it seems fitting to observe that the announcement of the ecumenical council has aroused in every mind expectations, dreams, curiosity, utopias, velleities of every kind, and countless fantasies. Even among the faithful the expectation of the Council has awakened a great many desires and hopes.[21]

This state of expectancy is warranted, and in fact does honor to those who entertain it. We can expect great things of the Council: grace, enlightenment, and spiritual vitality, as well as a renewal in discipline and worship, in the administration of the Church in its relation with the modern world and its approach to separated christians.

31. Yet we must avoid nourishing capricious, strictly personal and arbitrary wishes. We must not expect the Council to conform to our particular views; on the contrary, it is we who must enter into the general views of the Council. To believe that the Council will repair our human frailty, and that it will immediately bring perfection into the Church and the world, is an ingenuous dream. It is asking too much to expect the ecumenical council to remedy the manifold practical inconveniences and even the manifold theoretical imperfections of Catholic life that each one of us may encounter in his experience as a member or observer of ecclesiastical society. It is also asking far too much to expect the Council to realize such beautiful ideas as might arise in the mind of every single christian or particular religious group.

32. It might be useful to remember that the Council has also been prepared magnificently through assembling the suggestions of the whole Church. All the bishops, all the Roman congregations, all the religious orders, all the Catholic universities and a vast number of experts, men and women, scholars and men of practical experience, ecclesiastics and

---

21. Cf. "Ils attendent le Concile," *Témoignage chrétien*, Paris, 1961; *Qu'attendons-nous du Concile?* Bruxelles, 1960. "Un Concile pour notre temps," R. Voillaume in *Ce que le monde attend de l'Église et du Concile*, pp. 29-57 (Paris: Ed. du Cerf, 1961); P. Lombardi, S.J., *Il Concilio, per una riforma nella carita* (Roma: Apes, 1961); Hans Küng, *The Council, Reform and Reunion*, translated by Cecily Hastings (New York: Sheed and Ward, 1961).

laymen—all have been consulted and given freedom to express whatever they thought and desired for the welfare of religion and of the Church. Furthermore, many thick volumes have been published, gathering and systematizing this enormous material for the use of the council fathers now, and for the gradual improvement and modernization of the clergy's life later.

Never before has a council been so extremely and accurately prepared. Undoubtedly the Council has been blessed with a wealth of advice, experiences and aspirations. Through the debates and deliberations of the great conciliar assembly the whole Church, we may say, has contributed arguments in support of its faith, piety and love of Christ.

This must edify and comfort us immensely, for such is our Church! Here we see how the entire Catholic world, in its authorized spokesmen and at given periods in its history, expresses its freedom. And even more we see here how it is invited to express itself and present, in a competent and responsible way, desires and judgments of all sorts. A whole literature on the forthcoming Council has been growing spontaneously; another is sure to spring up upon its conclusion. And so we can see that the Catholic Church's so-called dogmatism does not suffocate but rather excites the thoughts of all the Church's teachers and disciples. It is the worship of truth proper to God's holy Church that makes this phenomenon possible, and that asserts itself as a great living choir whose countless voices never degenerate into a babel-like confusion.

33. From this very moment the conductor of this great living choir, the Pope, has furnished the Ecumenical Council with two fundamental themes: the inner reform of ecclesiastical life and the search for ways of reconciling our separated brothers within the Church's Catholic unity. Here are his own words: "They will consider, in particular, the growth of the Catholic faith, the restoration of sound morals among the

christian flock, and appropriate adaptation of Church discipline to the needs and conditions of our times.

"This event will be a wonderful spectacle of truth, unity and charity. For those who behold it but are not one with the Apostolic See, we hope that it will be a gentle invitation to seek and find that unity for which Jesus Christ prayed so ardently to his Father in heaven."[22]

The Concept of the Reform of Christian Life

34. And so there arises in our minds the concept, so easy yet so difficult, of the reform of ecclesiastical life. But this time it is the Pope who raises the problem before the entire Church. Reform is a program for saints and a trumpet call for rebels. It elicits the naiveté of utopians and the empty proposals of politicians; the deepest need of contemplatives and pastors, and the undisciplined caprice of restless and stubborn spirits. Throughout the centuries reform has been from time to time the ferment that has renewed the Catholic tradition, just as it has been a ferment that has dissolved the ecclesiastical structure.

Those familiar with the Church's history do in fact know the importance and dynamism that this concept has had in the history of Christianity throughout the centuries. It is enough to remember the great religious and political crisis which separated Protestants from the Catholic Church, called the Reformation, and the great effort to define doctrinal questions in that crisis and mend the moral evils at issue which was made by the Council of Trent and the subsequent movement of Catholic restoration, incorrectly called the Counter-Reformation. Yet in this whole effort we must not see simply a conservative defense-reaction, but a true and positive Catho-

22. Encyclical *Ad Petri Cathedram, A.A.S.,* 1959, p. 511. Also in *The Pope Speaks,* vol. 5, No. 4 (Autumn 1959), 369.

lic reform that has been blessing us with bountiful benefits from the ninetenth century until our own day.[23]

35. We must state this concept of reform precisely to ourselves because it is vital for understanding the aims of the Ecumenical Council and for penetrating its spirit. It is also very important because this concept is vigorously operative in the modern mind in different ways.

Where does the concept of reform come from? It springs from two sources: the identification of a given evil, and a reaction conceived in different ways. But here a specious objection arises: can there be evil in the Church? Is not the Church itself holy? Is it not infallible? The answer is simple for those who know how to perceive God's work in the Church: his design, his divine gifts of grace and truth, his final ends as they are directed to him and to eternal life. This work is holy, sanctifying and infallible both in its divine source, the Holy Spirit, and in some of its closely defined and qualified acts, such as solemn dogmatic definitions.

But God's work is embodied in men of this world who may be fallible and frail, even though sustained by grace and a commitment to follow Christ. We must distinguish, that is, two aspects in the Church: one, the Church as a divine institution; the other, the Church as a community made up of men. In a certain sense we might call the one ideal, the other real: one might be described in terms of the efficient, formal and final cause that constitutes God's work and is therefore perfect; the other in terms of the material cause—which is always, however, permeated by the formal cause—that is, its

23. A treatment of the historical manifestations of the concept of reform in the Church would be as long as the history of the Church itself, for reform is in fact part and parcel of its very life. As to the incubation of the concept of reform before the Council of Trent, cf. H. Jedin, *Storia del Concilio di Trento* (Brescia: Morcelliana, 1949), 14ff.

human composition that consists of imperfect men, sinners perhaps, though always sanctified by baptism.

The first aspect is the splendid and immaculate model of the Church that Christ conceived and loved as his mystical bride: "No stain," as St. Paul writes, "holy . . . spotless" (Eph 5:27). And yet this is not only a model, but a reality that is in process of actualization. In its historical and concrete form, it manifests the second aspect. Here we see mankind gathered together in the Church. Though militant and imperfect, it strives to perfect and sanctify itself according to the model, the idea that Christ conceived in respect to the glorious and eschatological Church—that is, the Church, beyond time, as it has reached its ultimate end.[24] Thus reform involves a perennial effort in the Church that aims to bring the divine idea close to human reality, and human reality close to the divine idea.

36. And so this our earthly Church, Christ's disciple in its human corporality and its sanctifying phase, is and ought to be in a state of continual and unrelenting reform. The Church's supernatural reality demands that its natural reality be a process of perennially striving for greater and greater perfection. When Jesus tells us, "But you are to be perfect, as your heavenly Father is perfect" (Mt 5:48) and when St. Paul urges us, "as God's favoured children, you must be like him" (Eph 5:1), and again urges us, "There must be a renewal in the inner life of your minds; you must be clothed in the new self . . ." (Eph 4:23-24), we are being invited to

---

24. Cf. Schnell, *Der Katholizismus als Prinzip des Fortschrittes,* 1897; Keppler *Ueber Wahre und falsche Reform,* 1930; Congar, *Vraie et fausse reforme dans l'Église* (Paris: Ed. du Cerf, 1950), pp. 92ff; De Lubac, *The Splendour of the Church,* pp. 55ff; Journet, *The Church of the Word Incarnate I* (p. 314 in the second revised French edition): "from this point of view it can be said that the visible Church can very well include sinners, but not sin." And cf. *ibid.,* pp. 124ff; Philips, *Pour un Christianisme adulte* (Paris: Casterman, 1962), pp. 167ff.

perfect ourselves in a process that will never be marked either by respite or limit. And we must live our lives in that state of continual moral tension which characterizes precisely the ascetic way of life here on earth, and which marks the Church's entire juridical discipline, moral education, ascetic and mystical practice. Reform is on the Church's regular agenda. Reform must never end.

37. But when we speak of reform in respect to an ecumenical council we usually think of serious, deep-rooted and widespread calamities and of some extraordinary measure for in fact this was the case at several previous councils. The present Council's distinctive mark, however, expressly oriented as it is toward some notable reform, originates in the fact that it has been convened through a desire to achieve good rather than escape evil. As a matter of fact today, through God's mercy, there are neither errors nor scandals nor deviations nor abuses such as demand the extraordinary measure of convening a Council.

Today, always through God's grace and the merit of so many good and holy christians, the Church finds itself in a state of suffering and weakness rather than in a condition of scandal and decadence. Its general and external aspect reveals wounds rather than sins, needs rather than disbelief. All this makes us even more grateful and happy that the Pope himself, and with no external pressure, has proclaimed the Council's convocation. He has been spontaneously animated by love of Christ and by a desire to foster even more intensely the process of perfecting the Church. We shall therefore have a council of positive rather than punitive reforms, and of exhortation rather than anathemas.

38. The Church's needs therefore follow the desires that the Church's children must nourish in respect to the forthcoming Council. The needs become solemn wishes, hopes, prayers. This single psychological change in the collective opinion of Catholics already constitutes a positive result of

the Council, even before it has opened. Thus the Pope's optimism spreads throughout the entire Church, and the Church's sensibility deepens enormously. There is neither an anguished and existentialist morbidity nor a sterile and pharisaical criticism. On the contrary, this deepening sensibility is completely pervaded by a search for truth and a trust in the good.

On this the eve of the Council we all feel invited to join in a universal examination of conscience. And who is not conscious of some need, some improvement, some greater perfection in our Catholic religious life? This explains why so very many prognostications and proposals are gathering thickly around the Council from all quarters.[25]

Some Concrete Prospects

39. It seems to us instructive to invite our faithful to form an idea, even if a summary one, of the prospects that the Council opens up to far-seeing and good zealous souls. We shall simply give some rapid indications in order to broaden the horizon of the short-sighted individual. The collective aspirations of those who expect the Council to satisfy certain narrow personal interests, certain special and questionable preferences or certain fanciful utopias that readily take shape in minds which are sound though insufficiently experienced in reality also need enlarging. We would like to furnish your desires and prayers with a purpose that will make it more likely and more desirable that they be fulfilled.

25. On the efflorescence of desires with respect to the Council the following works may be consulted (among the very many published): *Umfrage zum Konzil* (Freiburg i.B.: Herder, 1961); this is a collection of 81 opinions of laymen and theologians on the tasks of the forthcoming Council; *Fragen an das Konzil* (Freiburg i.B.: Herder, 1961); Henry Daniel-Rops, *The Second Vatican Council; the Story behind the Ecumenical Council of Pope John XXIII,* translated by Alastair Guinan (New York: Hawthorn Books, 1962); cf. *Civiltà Cattolica,* years 1960, 1961, 1962; cf. preceding note 24; cf. various authors, *Il mondo attende la Chiesa* (Rome: Ed. Studium, 1957).

At the outset then let us state that some of these prospects concerning the Council refer to the Church's internal problems, and some to its external problems: that is to say, to those relations that the Church must bring up to date and restore.

40. What should be done within the Church? How pregnant with answers this one question is! One thing alone is desirable above everything else: to bring about an even closer union with Christ—with the Gospel's Christ: to know and imitate him, and yearn for his grace. Here we have a return to the sources and a proof of the Church's fidelity and authenticity. We must hope that the Church's whole life will grow, and that it will perfect and adorn itself with the mystery that it already does possess and live: the mystery, that is, of its real derivation from Jesus as the Gospels present him to us, as the age-old doctrinal meditation of the Church's magisterium and devotion has authoritatively outlined it from scriptural and traditional sources. In the Council the Church fulfills a great act of love towards Christ, for it is the thoroughly faithful bride rejoicing in her happiness.

41. Though this great act of love commemorates the historical Christ, it immediately turns to the heavenly Christ. It pushes on spontaneously to its living and divine reality and looks ahead to its future encounter. It becomes an expectation, invokes the Christ to come and engenders a spiritual, mystical élan. It becomes a hope that is already in part a joy, and that at the same time produces an ascetic tension, a presentiment, a watchfulness—a moral intensification that truly invests christian life today with the stamp of a pilgrimage towards the final end. And thus it is that the whole of human experience is classified and used in terms of its ultimate supernatural relationship: what is its value for eternal life?[26]

---

26. Cf. St. Bernard, *Ecclesia ante et retro oculata,* with a commentary by Father Congar in a lecture to Unesco, May 14, 1961, in *Informations Catholiques.*

42. From this survey of the Council's prospects, polarized as they are around Christ, the transition to the vision of Christ's mystical body is easy. The Council offers the Church a mirror in which to know and contemplate itself. It is common knowledge that what everybody is most eager to know is what the Council will say about the Church itself, for its constitutional law is still neither entirely clear nor exactly defined.

It is common knowledge that Vatican Council I did define this constitutional law in reference to the pope, and did recognize in St. Peter's successor to Rome's episcopal see not only pastoral functions for the City's diocese but primatial functions as a teacher who is universal and, when speaking *ex cathedra,* infallible. It also recognized in St. Peter's successor a pastor invested with full authority over the whole Church.[27] Yet, though it did affirm the harmonious relationship between the pope's primacy of power and that of the bishops, it had no time, on account of the political events in Rome in 1870, to define the constitutional law governing the bishops.

The interruption of the work of Vatican Council I and the need to clarify the episcopacy's essence, functions, powers and obligations leads us to believe that the episcopacy will be one of the topics to be treated at Vatican Council II. Thus we believe that an effort will be made to clarify the bishops' evangelical origins, their sacramental gifts of grace, their teaching, pastoral and jurisdictional powers, both in the single person of the bishop and in the collegial expressions. We further believe that an effort will be made to confirm at one and the same time the episcopacy's dependence on the pope and its communion, brotherhood and collaboration with him. From a doctrinal as well as a juridical and pastoral point of view the problem of the episcopacy is perhaps the

27. Cf. "Constitution" *Pastor Aeternus* of Vatican Council I, Denziger, n. 1828.

most eagerly awaited and the most weighty, as well as the most fecund with beneficial results.[28]

43. And the debate on the nature and function of the episcopacy in harmony with the Roman papacy may lead to a fresh and spontaneous affirmation of both the juridical and living unity of a Church assembled around St. Peter's See. It may also initiate, without any motives of recrimination, a greater and more organic internationalization of the Church's central government.

44. It thus seems likely that the Council's possible treatment of the episcopacy may also entail a similar treatment of the priesthood and the religious state, as well as virginity, perhaps, the conjugal state and the christian family.

45. We also believe that the Catholic laity will receive explicit and honorable recognition at the Council.

The layman in the Church will undoubtedly be raised to the level to which baptism and confirmation lift him: baptism by taking him up into the supernatural life, confirmation by summoning him to a public profession of his faith and to christian perfection. The terms of the simple layman's "royal priesthood" will be luminously clarified.

Let us hope, furthermore, that reference will be made to two forms of Catholic life regarding the layman's adult vocation: first, his intense, virile and appropriate spiritual life, shaped by means of an ever more intimate and cohesive participation in the liturgical mysteries of the christian community; secondly, his vocation (that has by now become official) to cooperate with the hierarchical apostolate so that even he,

---

28. Colson, *L'Evêque dans les communautes primitives tradition paulinienne et tradition johannique de l'épiscopat des origines à saint Irénee* (Paris: Ed. du Cerf, 1951); Dejaifve, *op. cit.;* Porrell, *La Théologie de l'Episcopat au premier Concile du Vatican* (Paris: Ed. du Cerf, 1961); R. Aubert, "L'Ecclesiologie du Concile du Vatican," in the volume *Le Concile et les Conciles* (Paris: Ed. du Cerf, 1960); C. Colombo, "Episcopato e Primato pontificio nella vita della Chiesa," in *Scuola Cattolica,* 1960.

the layman, may infuse fresh moral and religious vitality into the corporate body of the faithful, and may learn how to bear witness, in his own distinctive way, to Christ and the Church in the modern world.[29]

If what we suggest should come about, the human life that Christ has raised to the supernatural state will be amply and completely treated by the Council, and will appear to us in its sublime dignity and reborn beauty.

46. These considerations make us curious about other prospects, and most of all about faith. Beyond what we have already indicated to be our hope, will the Council furnish some new teaching about revealed truths, any new dogma?

This we cannot know, and this in itself indicates that the Council is not likely to define any new dogma as part of revelation.

On the other hand, a widespread consciousness in the Church seems to desire some wise admonition, some loving suggestion as to how we should and can preserve, deepen and profess our faith, the faith that is the source of our salvation and the one aspect of our heritage that is most threatened by the mentality shaped by modern errors of thought and morals.

47. Then there are the prospects concerning the Church's law (that is, canon law) and the prospects concerning practical provisions by which ecclesiastical authority governs the Church's visible body, that is, the community composed of the clergy, religious and laymen.

Concerning this chapter we may expect many innovations. The Pope himself already anounced them when, in connection with the opening of the Council, he declared his intention of submitting to a general revision the entire code of canon law that Pope Benedict XV promulgated in 1917. Here juridical science will find an extraordinary development that will get under way after the Council has ended (that is,

29. G. Philips, *op. cit.* The whole book deserves to be studied.

only after the Council has established the criteria for the revision).

We may anticipate that a great many of these reforms will hardly be noticed by the majority of the faithful, especially because the Church, as we were saying, will be unable to change either its fundamental structures or its traditional physiognomy. For it will not be able to break its consistency with its own legislation that interprets the evangelical spirit—as, for example, the clergy's celibacy. But it is believed that more than a few innovations will be introduced by the Council and noticed favorably by the faithful, too. These innovations will be in the liturgical, pastoral and missionary fields where concessions to the apostolic ministry are sure to be made.

48. There has been talk of an "aggiornamento" that the Council should bring into the concepts and norms that regulate the Church's life. What does "aggiornamento" mean: that the Church has been mistaken in its tactics until now? that the Church is archaic and behind the times? that the Church is conditioned by external events? that everything concerning it is open to discussion? that the Church can find its reason for being and flourish only if it moves in step with the natural evolution of secular history?

Clearly, the problems we are now raising are serious. Let us consider one, the problem of the Church's adaptation to the age and environment in which it finds itself living, an adaptation that in many respects the Church not only undergoes but actually desires and fosters. This capacity for adaptation is a function of its catholicity in time and among the nations of the world. It is a capacity for accepting man as he is, provided he conforms to God's natural and positive law, a capacity for filling him with its spirit of truth and grace. But this adaptation is not absolute, nor does it attack the primary and eternal values that the Church bears in itself and offers to mankind.

The relativism that its pastoral activity assumes in history is a symptom neither of weakness nor of senility. On the contrary, it is the product of an inner vigor, forever springing up anew, forever flourishing anew. Now would be a good time to study this question of the Church's eternal youth, but for the moment we must remain satisfied with the hope that we will see a concrete and splendid exemplification of it in the forthcoming Council.

49. This innovating aspect of the forthcoming Council is therefore as propitious as possible for reawakening a sense of good will in the whole Church. This Council instills no fear, even though it is justified in reserving its anathemas for error and evil. On the contrary, it arouses hope and love. This in fact explains why so very many people are looking forward to the great event.

Each one of us must look at the Council with desire and trust, for we are all interested in its successful outcome. Yet we must all be on our guard against two illusions that could tomorrow be turned into delusions. We should see the forthcoming Council within the larger framework of the Church's historical and traditional economy, rather than project it on the screen of either our own personal fantasies or personal desires.

The first illusion consists in thinking that the Council will decree reforms in the Church's existing law so radical and astonishing that they will alter its centuries-old features, transforming it into an institution entirely new and, as some say, modern—modelled, that is, on the juridical forms distinctive of contemporary associative life. But it will not do this.

The Church's present juridical structure certainly does need a few retouches, though it cannot be substantially changed. It does not betray Christ's genuine thought; it does not engender conditions of decadence and disintegration. On the contrary, it is the product of an historical experience that has been fostered by a rigorous intention of remaining faithful to and in harmony with the will and mind of the Church's divine founder. It also involves a natural and often loving concern for ways of approaching the effective and honorable structures of human society, as well as a humanistic tendency that religion displays as it celebrates the word of God made man. Furthermore, this structure has been tested in its essential lines by a magnificent testimony of wisdom and holiness, even when the human structure has assumed perhaps excessive or inopportune proportions. The Council will not alter the Catholic Church's traditional features. It will rather restore, we hope, its logical and original exigencies, and lead them to its beautiful and truly christian form.

50. The other illusion consists in believing that the Council will remedy the vast number of defects, imperfections and abuses that we ourselves encounter in Catholic life today. Undoubtedly the Council will seek to repair whatever imperfections do exist in every area of Catholic life. It is for a very good reason that all those competent to propose wise suggestions have been consulted, and commissions and subcommissions have been organized to reduce the suggestions to formulations capable of practical achievement.

Yet the Council is no magic and immediate panacea. Yes, the Council will issue programs involving a revision of discipline and worship in the Church. It will issue decrees and precepts involving the many areas that need to be corrected, brought up to date and developed. Yet its immediate greatness, even its effectiveness, will not consist in this. Nor will the Council be measured purely by the success of its juridical and liturgical results. It must be seen as a moment of the ineffable presence of God's loving and merciful action in his Church.

For above all the Council will call upon the Holy Spirit to enliven the whole Church more vigorously. It will allow faith to express itself in a unanimous, solemn and triumphant way. It will advance great ideas and great principles of christian living to be derived from a fresh and passionate study of the Gospel, and from a study of the wisdom that borrowed its light and developed from the Gospel. This it will do: it will breathe into the Church a fresh consciousness, a fresh energy, a fresh commitment, a fresh charity.

It will give the Church an intimate consciousness of what it is and of what it must do. From this profound and inner experience it will draw a fresh power of expressing itself: in preaching, in the apostolate, in bearing witness, in suffering, in goodness, in art, in holiness. But none of this produces an immediate result, nor is it entirely visible. What is more, the result will not depend on the Council alone; it will depend on the whole mystical body that is the Church. It will depend on us, too—on each one of us. We must all therefore commit ourselves, from this very moment, to accept the Council's directives in prompt and filial obedience.

51. This sublime and in part mysterious finality of the forthcoming Council is outlined for us in the inspired words of Pope John XXIII himself, who teaches:

Everything that the new Ecumenical Council is to do is really aimed at restoring to full splendor the simple and pure lines that the face of the Church of Jesus had at its birth, and at presenting it as its Divine Founder made it: "without blemish or wrinkle." Its journey through the centuries is still a long way from the point where it will be transported into an eternity of triumph. So the highest and noblest aim of the Ecumenical Council (whose preparation is just now beginning and for whose success the whole world is praying) is to pause a little in a loving study of the Church and try to rediscover the lines of her more fervent youth, to reconstruct them in a way that will reveal their power over modern minds that are tempted and deceived by the false theories of the prince of this world, the open or hidden adversary of the Son of God, Redeemer and Savior.[30]

The Impact of the Council on Society and the World

52. What we have just said may be rounded out by another extremely important prospect that the Council opens up. This concerns the Council's impact outside the Catholic Church—its impact, that is, on the contemporary world.

The world as such has no practical relationship with this great ecclesiastical event. Unlike what has happened in the past,[31] up even to the time of the Council of Trent, civil authority is entirely removed from the scene today. The process involving the progressive distinction and separation of Church and State excludes any participation whatsoever by civil society in the Council itself. This separation also excludes any interference by worldly powers and temporal interests in the course of this magnificent event, at once human and religious. And let us note that it is in this fact of non-interference that modern secularism finds one of its expressions.

The Church stands alone in celebrating the Council. The Church, God forbid, might be obstructed or disturbed in the course of such a moment. This did in fact occur in the course of Vatican Council I. But, thanks to God, as we were saying (n. 21), the Church remains independent.

53. Yet by the nature of things the Council must also establish precise relations with secular society. It is a very great historical event, a great human and visible phenomenon, an affirmation of principles and laws, a fount of factors influencing thought and morals, and such a great concentration of international representatives that even the surrounding world must in some way become conscious of this singular event, and may even derive some profit from it.

30. *The Pope Speaks,* vol. 7, No. 1 (1961), 65-66.
31. Hefele, I, introduction, *passim.* On the *Concilia mixta,* cf. "Conciles" in *Dictionnaire de Théologie Catholique.*

The Church and its Universal Salvific Mission

54. The Council does not wish to relate itself to the modern world simply because it finds itself so related in point of fact. It rather sets out to relate itself to the world deliberately. The Pope has said this repeatedly in a tone so splendid that it seems to echo the Bible's ancient prophecies. Let us listen, for example: ". . . truly Christ's Church expects abundant fruits from this event that wishes to serve truth, to be an act of charity and an example of peace proclaimed to all peoples from this sublime chair . . ."[32]

And in the bull announcing the Council we hear:

Even though the main goal toward which the Church is striving is not an earthly one, still, as she journeys along her path, she cannot ignore the questions that have to do with temporal goods or pay no attention to the labors that produce these goods. She is well aware of the precise benefit that can be conferred on immortal souls by whatever serves to make a little more human the lives of individual men, whose eternal salvation she is seeking. She realizes that when she sheds the light of Christ upon men, she is helping them to know themselves better. For she leads them to understand what they really are, what dignity they enjoy, what goal they must pursue.

As a result, at the present time the Church is, either officially or unofficially, playing a role in international organizations and has developed an organized social teaching which touches on families, schools, employment, human society and its various ties, and all questions of this kind; and because of this doctrine, the Church has achieved so lofty a pinnacle of prestige that her solemn pronouncements are treated with the highest respect by all prudent men, who regard her as a spokesman and defender for morality and a vindicator of the rights and duties of individuals and of nations.[33]

32. From the allocution for the Consistory, January 16, 1961.
33. The Bull *Humanae Salutis,* Christmas 1961; also in *The Pope Speaks,* vol. 7, No. 4, 358. Cf. C. Colombo, "La indizione del Concilio Ecumenico Vaticano II," *Vita e Pensiero,* January 1962, 2-6.

55. Hence the Church, through the forthcoming Council, plans to come into contact with the world. Let us ponder this well, for we are in the presence of a great act of charity. The Church will not only think of itself. It will think of all men as it remembers that it is the continuation of Christ, the Word incarnate, who came into the world to save it in whatsoever state it might be found.[34]

For this purpose it will seek to become sister and mother to all men. It will seek to be poor, simple, humble and lovable in its language and way of life. For this purpose it will seek to make itself understood, and to give contemporary man the opportunity of hearing it and of speaking to it in simple and every-day language. For this purpose it will repeat to the world its wise words of human dignity, loyalty, freedom, love, moral earnestness, courage and sacrifice. For this purpose, as we were saying, it will take care to "bring itself up to date." It will divest itself, if necessary, of any old royal cloak still remaining on its sovereign shoulders, so that it may clothe itself with the simpler forms demanded by modern taste.

For this purpose it will summon laymen, its good and faithful Catholic laymen, to serve as a bridge linking its supernatural and religiously sanctioned sphere to the sociological and temporal sphere in which they themselves live. It will summon them, and as it were delegate them, in the light of their willing and competent cooperation, to undertake the arduous yet sublime work of the *consecratio mundi;*[35] of permeating, that is, the immense sphere of the secular world with christian principles and solid natural and supernatural virtues.

34. Cf. Y. Congar: The Church "does not exist to be very beautiful. Looking in the mirror, it does not say, 'How beautiful I am. I am the Lord's bride. I am a queen.' The Church exists *propter nos et propter nostram salutem.*" In "Une, Sainte, Catholique et Apostolique," *Un Concile pour Notre Temps* (Paris: Ed. Cerf, 1961), p. 244.
35. Cf. Pius XII, *Discorsi,* III, 460; XIII, 295; XV, 590, etc.

56. Will this powerful and marvellous effort succeed? Will the world understand that an institution exists on earth that entertains no other aim than to make it good, sound, peaceful and happy? Will the world understand that its agnosticism, its materialism, its atheism must finally be overcome by a courageous and wise rediscovery of God and Christ? Will the world remain silent in the face of the great invitation that the Church is sure to extend so that they—the world and the Church—may pray together? In the excitement of a fresh and revealing spiritual experience, will it at least respond with a hesitant amen? Will this triumphant hymn to the God of the universe, to the Christ of true civilization, resound again on earth?

57. We may be allowed to hope that this will come about. We must at least desire that it come about with all our heart. We must pray for it and work for its achievement: first, by making our own profession of the christian faith profound and sincere; and secondly, by seeking in every way to invigorate and spread it. And so we find ourselves on the Council's highest peak.

Let us listen to the Pope:

In the modern period the face of the world has changed profoundly and it is hard for it to keep its balance between the attractions and the perils of a constant and almost exclusive pursuit of material goods, and in the midst of a total neglect or watering down of the supernatural, spiritual principles that characterized the implanting and spread of Christian civilization through the centuries. In this modern period, the question is not so much one of some particular point or other of doctrine or of discipline that has to be brought back to the pure fonts of Revelation and of tradition, as it is of restoring the substance of humane and Christian thinking and living (for which the Church has served as custodian and teacher through the centuries) to full force and to its proper splendor.

On the other hand, it is certainly important and even obligatory for us to deplore the errors and faults of a human spirit that is being tempted and pushed in the direction of concentrating completely on enjoyment of the earthly goods that modern scientific research now puts within the easy grasp of the man of our age. But may God keep us from exaggerating the extent of this to the point of making ourselves believe that God's heavens have now closed over our head once and for all, that, as a matter of fact, "darkness has covered the whole earth," and that there is nothing left for us to do but shed tears as we plod along our difficult path.

Instead, we must take courage.[36]

Thus the Pope, with his invigorating optimism, exhorts and comforts us. He wishes to prepare us, it seems, for a Council in which evil and error will be deplored, but in which the good will be sustained rather than anathemas launched against erring men. The alienated, too, will be considered and loved.

The Call of Charity and Unity to Our Separated Brothers

58. We are thus led to reflect for a moment on that vast and multi-dimensional category of brothers who are christians, still privileged to bear such a great name though separated from the unity of the Catholic Church. It is an extremely delicate and complex problem yet, as we all know, the Pope has boldly and lovingly proposed that it be taken up at the forthcoming Council, since he first announced its convocation in his address to the Sacred College in the great hall of St. Paul's monastery, on January 25, 1959. On that occasion he stated openly that the Ecumenical Council should not only aim at "edifying the whole christian people." It should also "invite again all the faithful of the separated communities" to follow it "lovingly in the search for that unity and grace yearned for by so many people from all points of the globe."

59. We cannot dwell on this problem for the moment. But every year, during the octave of Church unity, we devote ourselves to it with great zeal and treat it thoroughly and thought-

36. Address to the Preparatory Commissions of the Council, November 14, 1960; in *The Pope Speaks,* vol. 6, No. 4 (1960), 378-379.

fully. For the moment it is enough for us to bear in mind that this problem, so extremely difficult yet so important and urgent, does constitute one of the principal objects among the several envisaged by the Council. Most likely, however, a solution of the problem will remain beyond the Council's reach. Perhaps we have not yet earned so great a miracle, though the Ecumenical Council may prepare the solution for which we all so deeply yearn. In this respect the Council will be of a preparatory nature; it will be a Council of longing.

And God will that all of us Catholics may be able to engender in ourselves this real and operative spirit! We must hope that God will grant our tearful prayer that unity among christians may be re-established around Peter and the Apostles in communion with him!

We must hope that we may help modify the opinion of dissidents concerning the Pope and the Catholic Church! We must hope that we may know how to receive the separated christians honorably and in a spirit of true brotherhood, should they appear on the threshold of their home and ours, the Catholic Church! We must wish to understand them better and to appreciate all the truth and the good that still remains in their religious heritage! We must in fact hope and pray that the Council will overcome the obstacles that obstruct the one and only way to the happiest of all meetings. This is the way of faith: that is, of the reality of Christ's one, true religion.

May the Council loosen the bonds of so many sorrowful memories of the past. Through discussions of historical exegesis that also involve honor and prestige, these memories still obstruct the dynamics that are necessary at a particular moment to resolve the great problem. Finally, may the Council enflame our hearts with greater charity—for it is charity, in the last resort, that will move us towards the crucial meetings.

60. Consequently, if the forthcoming Council should un-

fortunately fail to go beyond a desire and preparation for the future ecumenical reconciliation within the Church's unity, it will undoubtedly be a prelude to a future council. And one that might celebrate the feast of all christians finally united as brothers in one flock and under one Pastor![37]

61. All these general considerations should oblige each one of us to reflect, and to develop our own understanding of the Ecumenical Council's real and profound meaning to the extent of our capacities. Men have called the Council many things: the chief moment of God's loving action in the government of the Church; the most salient religious affirmation in a world that is losing the sense of religion; the great hour in which the Church finds itself anew; the greatest effort of Catholicism to understand, attract, vivify the contemporary world; the total and modern joining of apostolic and missionary forces; the proclamation of the principles on which, as on a cornerstone, the modern world may find stability, peace and progress; the Church's most exacting commitment and fidelity to Christ and his saving mission.

The variety itself of these attempts at a synoptic opinion about the Council indicates the greatness of the event, and the event itself engenders one of our very first duties: to think about the Council.[38]

37. Cf. Prof. Nicola Jaeger, *Il Romano Pontefice, Il Concilio Ecumenico ed i Lontani* (Varese, 1959); Hans Küng, *The Council, Reform and Reunion*, translated by Cecily Hastings (New York: Sheed and Ward, 1961); Dumont, *Les Voies de l'unité chrétienne* (Paris: Ed. du Cerf, 1954); cf. English trans. by Henry St. John, O.P., *Approaches to Christian Unity* (Baltimore: Helicon, 1959); Schlier, Volk, DeVries, *Unité de l'Église et tâche oecuménique* (Paris: Ed. de l'Orante, 1961); Decarreaux, "Catholiques et Orthodoxes devant le problème de l'unité," in *Revue des deux Mondes*, June 15, 1959; Cardinal Léger, "Chrétiens désunis," Pastoral Letter, Montreal, 1962.

38. Cf. the collective letter of the Dutch bishops: "Le sens du Concile" (Paris: Ed. du Cerf); L. Jaeger (Archbishop of Paderborn), *Das oekumenische Konzil, die Kirche und Christenheit*, 1960 (cf. English trans. by A. V. Littledale, *The Ecumenical*

The Range of Our Concrete Commitment

62. Additional duties arise from this great event. Let us simply sketch out a few in an elementary fashion.

1) Let us endeavor to be informed about the forthcoming Ecumenical Council. This is in fact the chief aim of this our pastoral letter. The Council is a great event, an event that concerns each one of us. Today books, articles and lectures treat this matter extensively. Let us all endeavor to be well informed about it. Pastors, teachers, priests, leaders of Catholic associations and writers are all exhorted to give the Council the widest possible publicity.

2) Let us all try to understand, collectively and individually, how we may, and should, contribute to the Council's success as it sums up the spirit of the whole christian people. Hence at this time each one of us must reawaken his act of faith and shape his own christian life in the best possible way. The renewal that we are awaiting from the Council must begin today, in the way we have suggested, and it must begin with us. And so in fact the Pope exhorts us: "Beloved sons! We do not hesitate to say that all of our cares and efforts to make the Council a great success might well be in vain if this collective effort at sanctification were not whole-hearted and universal. Nothing can make as much of a contribution to it as the quest for and the achievement of holiness. The prayers and virtues of individuals, and their interior spirit become an instrument of immense good . . ."[39]

Council, the Church and Christendom [London: G. Chapman, 1961]); Cardinal Frings, "Vatican Council II in the Face of Modern Thought," address of November 20, 1961; various authors, *I Concili nella vita della Chiesa* (Milano: Vita e Pensiero, 1961); various authors, *Il Concilio Ecumenico* (Milano: Vita e Pensiero, 1961); cf. also the Pastoral Letters of the Archbishop of Avignon, the Archbishop of Cambrai, etc.

39. From the allocution for the celebration of the liturgy of the Byzantine-Slav rite in St. Peter's, November 13, 1960.

The Pope has invited everyone—intellectuals, children, those who suffer, priests[40]—to contribute to the Council by preparing themselves for it, each in his own distinctive way. Every class, every person can feel the invitation as if it were addressed to him personally: it is the whole christian community that must work together spiritually and morally for the successful outcome of the event.

3) The simplest and easiest way of offering our spiritual tribute is to pray for it. In fact we have already directed that a special prayer be added to all ferial masses, a prayer to the Holy Spirit for the intention of the Council. We also recommend that frequent mention be made of this great event at public functions and in private prayers. The prayer that the Holy Father has prescribed for this purpose may well suggest to us joyful words and sentiments.

"To Feel With the Church and the Pope"

63. Let us conclude by recalling that both our patron saints, Ambrose and Charles, are linked to solemn moments in the history of the Church's councils.

As defender of the faith at Nicea and as president of the Council of Aquileia (not to mention other similar activities), Saint Ambrose shows us how great a trust he held in this solemn manifestation of the Church's life. Saint Charles too, although he was in Rome, made a great contribution to the successful outcome of the Council of Trent. And while he was in Milan, through diocesan synods and provincial councils and his own unceasing and unsurpassed pastoral work he did everything possible to put into effect the decrees of the Council of Trent, and apply them to the life of his people. Both these men teach us, especially us their belated though

---

40. See the passages from pontifical addresses cited by Mons. S. Garofalo, *La grande ora della Chiesa e del mondo* (Roma: Ed. Paoline).

by no means ungrateful children, how great an account we must take of the Council for which we are preparing ourselves.

May their protection, with the ever invoked intercession of our Lady, make us worthy of "feeling with the Church and the Pope" the forthcoming historical event. And may it also make us capable of reaping from it, both for ourselves and for the entire world, a rich harvest of spiritual fruit.

May our pastoral benediction confirm these prayers.

Ecumenical Councils in an International Historical Framework

*The Importance of an Historical Event
and its Impact on the World*

The forthcoming ecumenical Vatican Council II that Pope John XXIII has convened is an important event in the life of the Catholic Church. This opinion has been expressed in so many ways by so many people, we may rightly say that in this respect public opinion is, if not perfectly, then at least sufficiently well informed, especially on its highest and most alert levels such as the one I am honored to address today.

On the other hand, what importance an ecumenical council might have outside the Catholic Church is difficult to assess. It is therefore a question that merits our attention, since no matter how the event is assessed it does assume international, indeed world proportions. For it interests many men who are invested with a special authority and are endowed with considerable culture, such as ecclesiastical prelates, members of the forthcoming Council. It also concerns a great many other men, the faithful, who will attach great weight to the Council itself and its achievements, both doctrinal and practical—a weight that will be felt even beyond the society of believers, in the secular world, in civil society.

Consequently, the impact of the Ecumenical Council on the contemporary world is a worthy topic for an Institute for Studies in International Politics that is attentive to the salient facts of contemporary life. If it is eager to assess them within an historical framework that is not confined to immediate events but embraces vast evolutionary cycles of human civilization; if such an Institute is fully aware of the spiritual forces that influence the life of peoples in a powerful if not altogether coercive way at times, this Institute, we say, is well equipped to realize its aim of studying the meaning and value of ecumenical councils—and especially, as far as possible, the forthcoming one. For it does not aim at studying the councils for their own sake, but rather at analyzing their impact on temporal society, on the life of nations, on the international community.

Allow me, then, to express my pleasure with the wisdom that this Institute displays concerning this subject too: for its study of the popularity and uniqueness of the event, its breadth, its contemporary relevance, its moral and spiritual character, its position in an age-old chain of similar events—not to mention the significant circumstance that it is being celebrated in Rome, now the capital of Italy, where Vatican Council I was suddenly interrupted when the popes' temporal power was ended in September, 1870.[1]

1. For the background, consult the following works: R. Aubert, "L'ecclésiologie du Concile du Vatican," in *Le Concile et Les Conciles* (Paris: Ed. du Cerf, 1960), pp. 245-284; R. Aubert, *Le Pontificat de Pie IX* (Paris: Bloud et Gay, 1952), p. 311ff; E. Cecconi, *Storia del Concilio ecumenico Vaticano* (Roma: 1878), I, II, etc.; O. Dejaifve, S.J., *Pape et Evêques au premier Concile du Vatican* (Paris: Desclée de Brouwer, 1960); H. Jedin, *Ecumenical Councils of the Catholic Church: An Historical Outline,* translated by Ernest Graf (New York: Herder & Herder, 1960), (Page references are to the Italian edition [Roma: Herder, 1960], p. 198ff); A. Oddone, S.J., *Concili ecumenici e vicende*

I must therefore say something about the role that the ecumenical council has come to assume in contemporary international life.

The Relations between the Council and Civil Society

The first observation to be made in this connection is that the role which the forthcoming Ecumenical Council will play in relation to civil society today differs from the role that previous ecumenical councils assumed in the civil society of their age.

Today we can say that the Council—this extraordinary and, in certain respects, greatest event in the Catholic Church's life—has no connection whatsoever with civil society. The cardinals, bishops, abbots and prelates with canonic jurisdiction, the superiors general of exempt congregations of religious of the whole world, all will gather around the Pope, without whom a council can claim no ecumenical character. They will number, should all come, some five thousand persons.[2] All these men will discuss religious and moral, liturgical and pastoral questions, and will study the great and complex problems relative to the reintegration of the separated churches—Eastern, Protestant and Anglican—within the Catholic Church. They will issue rules and instructions affecting missionary expansion in the world, both to civilized peoples alien to christianity and to peoples currently in evolutionary ferment. They will be concerned about the consequent penetration of them by the fundamental christian principles that to such an extent are one and the same with those of our own civilization. They will also issue canons that will affect the human manifestations of Catholic life: that is, the life of priests, the religious, laymen, of social classes, the

---

del Concilio Vaticano (Milano: Vita e Pensiero, 1934); cf. Civiltà Cattolica, 1934, IV, 628.
2. Annuario Pontificio, 1313-1314.

family, and youth, as well as the salient phenomena of Catholic life itself, such as culture, education, art, entertainment. And they will define perhaps the criteria governing the relations between the Church and the modern State. These are some of the things that they will do. And yet civil society, and even the State itself, will completely ignore this episode in our contemporary history.

It will ignore it; that is to say, officially it will have nothing to do with it. Undoubtedly the diplomatic corps accredited to the Holy See, flanked perhaps by a few special missions delegated for the occasion, will attend the inaugural and peripheral ceremonies, and surely a host of newspaper men, photographers, artists, pilgrims and tourists will be present, though they will all remain outside the Conciliar assembly. And they will remain outside not only physically but effectively. That is to say, they will have no "voice in the chapter"; they will be unable to exercise any internal intervention or influence whatsoever.

We were pleased to hear the respectful words in reference to the forthcoming Council that the president of the Italian Council, Signor Fanfani, spoke when he presented his newly formed government to Parliament. We all value his words because they express and confirm the fact that the civil authority must, and in fact does, wish to remain outside the Council's internal proceedings.

The Church stands alone in celebrating its proceedings, and presents itself as clearly distinct from the State. The Church is a distinct society, perfect, independent, juridically autonomous, free. The distinction between Church and State has reached its full expression even in those cases where—as in Italy—there is no separation because the relations between the two societies have been solemnly and clearly defined by mutual agreement. Church and State remain two distinct societies. Each is sovereign in its own sphere and each endeavors, one way or another, to complement the other by providing the people whom they have in common with the means for their optimal development and for attaining the ends that are immanent to life itself. One society is supernatural, the other natural; one reaches beyond time, the other exists only in time.

This state of affairs is an extremely important achievement in our historical evolution. In itself it would constitute an endless theme for reflection if we wished to search for the ideal principles that engender and vigorously promote the two-fold process of reciprocal emancipation of Church and State. We should move from the historical and juridical to the philosophical sphere, and note how the Church's conception of mankind in general has led it to sharpen its distinction from the State. Nor should we forget that the Church has been and intends to be friendly to the *respublica*. It acknowledges its powers and competence, and aims at stabilizing its functions and promoting its welfare. But we should also observe that the anti-religious dialectic originates in secular thought. It is gradually incorporated into various political structures and activities, until it succeeds in some cases in transforming the distinction of the two societies first into a separation, then an opposition.

The current situation may thus be assessed in different ways, though one advantage it does undoubtedly offer: it obliges the Church to assume the native, essential form that its constitutional law outlines—or better, that Christ its divine founder has conceived in a sublime and pure ideal vision, which is his Church. Thus it might seem logical and respectful of the citizen, the politician, the layman, the ruler to be unconcerned with the Council as something that does not affect him at all.

But as we were saying, too precipitate and complete an unconcern would not be an intelligent position for the secularist, even if he should be satisfied with his ineligibility, and with remaining outside the Ecumenical Council. It would not be an intelligent position above all because historically this has not always been the case.

As the Church is about to celebrate one of the most serious and solemn moments in its life, this clear distinction that the Church makes against the interference and even participation of the civil power, however it may be represented, is something new, and therefore well worth noting.

Some will say that Vatican Council I also took place in the absence of any civil power. This is true, and it was the first time that it happened, after some twenty previous ecumenical councils. Yet Vatican Council I was burdened with troublesome and importunate polemics that Vatican Council II, it seems, should be able to avoid. Vatican Council I was born in an atmosphere of debate and even controversy, as its chief subject was the definition of the doctrine concerning papal infallibility. Some of its protagonists, even before the Council opened, were such distinguished men as Bishops Dupanloup and Maret, and Louis Veuillot of France, Bishop Nardi, Cardinal Manning of England, Bishop Hefele, and Professor Doellinger in Germany. The latter especially did not submit to the definition of the doctrine. In fact, in letters to Prince Hohenlohe then ruling in Bavaria, he sought to arouse civil authorities by instilling in them the fear of an "absolutist Church of Rome," against which he opposed "the ancient Catholic Church."

In France a disturbance was created in the legislative body through the intervention of Adolph Gueroult, in connection with a famous article that appeared in *Civiltà Cattolica* on February 6, 1869. This article published news that originated with the Apostolic Nuncio in France, Archbishop Chigi, and anticipated some possibilities about the impending Council. Adolph Gueroult disinterred the famous Declaration of the Gallican clergy, aroused fears about the predominance of the ecclesiastical power over the State, and attacked the policy of the government. In Italy things were more peaceful: neither the Menabrea government nor the government of Giovanni Lanza (December, 1869-July, 1873) had any desire either to create a bad impression on the bishops or to irritate the French, who then occupied Rome. On September 30, 1869, Minister of Justice Pironti sent a circular to the attorney general of the Courts of Appeal announcing that the King's government had no desire to interfere with the participation of bishops and other ecclesiastics in the assembly of the Council. Yet he made "an absolute exception for any subsequent resolution concerning anything that might violate the laws of the kingdom and the rights of the state."[3]

Nevertheless an anonymous pamphlet, written in bad French and published in April, 1869, in Florence (then the capital of the Italian government), propagated the most daring royalist ideas about the rights of the civil power concerning ecumenical councils. And it may help us to recall how these alleged rights were summed up: "The State possesses the right to participate in the proceedings [of an ecumenical council], indeed to initiate one on its own. It has the right to intervene in order to fix the time and place of the meeting; to attend not only all the sessions but also all the synodal meetings [that is to say, preparatory meetings], and to make itself heard. It has the right to a place of honor and to active participation in all the deliberations of the council. No resolution may be taken, nor can be valid, unless it is accepted and promulgated by the State. Bishops cannot go to a council without the State's permission; though the State may summon them in certain cases, and has the right to indicate who may attend. These are the State's privileges."[4] But nothing whatsoever came of this.

In fact, on May 26, 1869, Bismarck wrote Arnim, his ambassador in Rome, that "the whole participation of State au-

3. Cecconi, *op. cit.*, p. 662.
4. *Ibid.*, II, pp. 1453 and 1456.

thorities in a council rests on grounds that are entirely foreign and, for us, non-existent—on a conception of the relations between State and Church that belongs to the past.

"The French government (whose troops had guaranteed the existence of the Papal States since 1849), insisted on the French Emperor's right to be represented at the council. The claim was made in a speech by the Prime Minister, Ollivier, on July 10, 1869, but to the Pope's intense relief, Napoleon III refrained from the nomination of a conciliar envoy . . ."[5]

Thus Vatican Council I took place in absolute autonomy with respect to the civil power, and suffered no political interference whatsoever. But, as we were saying, this has not always been the case, though it is important to note so that we may understand how the forthcoming Council fits into the international sphere. An examination of the role that the State played in previous ecumenical councils, starting from the first, the Council of Nicea convened by Constantine in 321 a few years after the Edict of Milan, would constitute a very delicate and fascinating chapter of history.

Let us review rapidly. "The recently discovered fragments of Philostorgius," Battifol writes, "reveal the fact that the proposal to assemble a council of all the bishops for the sake of confirming the doctrine of the consubstantiality of the Word with the Father was made by the bishop of Alexandria, named Alexander; that he attracted the bishop of Cordova, Osius, to this project, which Constantine then adopted . . . The unity of the Empire that Constantine restored was providentially suited for a general council. Constantine was forced to accept the project of assembling the universal episcopacy into a council as a magnificent idea as well as the one effective means of achieving religious peace. Besides, it never entered his mind that the work of this ecclesiastical assembly could be done without the support of his own imperial sovereignty."[6]

5. Jedin, *op. cit.*, p. 200.
6. Battifol, *La Paix constantinienne*, p. 313ff.

Thus the ecumenical councils were born under the impulse and protection of the civil authority. And so Constantine said of himself: "I too am a bishop; you—addressing the clergy—are bishops for the Church's internal affairs, while I am the bishop that God has chosen to direct the Church's external affairs."[7] We know how this principle developed and how it immediately degenerated into caesaropapism with Constantius II. We also know the sort of doctrine that theologians, canonists and historians have derived from these words which are the source of a tradition that— in many different forms and degrees—has reached as far as the Council of Trent. This is the tradition of the double, indeed triple presidency of an ecumenical council. There is the real presidency, that consists in the internal direction of the assembly and its discussions; the purely formal and honorary presidency that is granted for special purposes; and the protective presidency, that consists in the exercise of the means necessary to maintain order and freedom among the Council's members, without interference in the subject matter under discussion.[8]

We do not intend to treat here of the so-called *concilia mixta,* in which the civil and ecclesiastical authorities met to discuss problems of interest to the State or the citizen.[9]

The Autonomy of Powers Affirmed by St. Ambrose and St. Charles

I cannot remain silent about our own St. Ambrose, the great doctor. As early as the fourth century—the first in which the Church appears, moves and asserts itself in public life— he grasped immediately the fundamental (I was about to say, modern) character of the principles that should govern the relations between Church and State. He immediately

7. Eusebius, *Vita Constantini,* 4, 24.
8. Cf. Hefele, *op. cit.,* I, p. 41, n. 3.
9. Cf. "Conciles," *Dictionnaire de Théologie Catholique.*

established in exact terms the question of the respective functions of Church and State, as well as matters concerning a council. Unlike what was occurring elsewhere, and especially in the East, he starts from "the great principle of the autonomy of the two powers, the spiritual and the temporal, and holds that while they both respect moral laws and both agree on questions of common interest they remain separate in their respective, independent spheres."[10]

He maintains that the *ordo ecclesiasticus* (that is, the hierarchy alone) is competent in matters of faith and matters regarding the Church's inner life, and is the first to advance the theory of the *jus sacerdotale*.[11]

In this respect Ambrose's action at the Council of Aquileia in 381 is typical. It is followed up by the well-known synodal letters *Benedictus, Provisum* and *Quamlibet* that he addressed to the Western Emperor Gratian, and *Sanctum* and *Fidei* that he addressed to Theodosius, who at that time was the Eastern Emperor. While he enlists the imperial authority in support of the Council's activity by invoking the assistance of the secular power, he vindicates the Church's spiritual freedom, indeed asserts its priority in the objective hierarchy of values (cf. *Ep.,* X, 12), for he is certain that "the State's duty to be faithful to God is one with its own interest."[12]

We could make similar observations about the other saint who marks the history of Milan, St. Charles Borromeo. As the young Secretary of State for Pope Pius IV he played a vital role in bringing the Council of Trent to an end. But the role that he played as a cardinal in relation to the policy of that Council (that is, in the relations with the State authorities of his time, then called princes), is less easy to express in terms of doctrinal positions, for it is a role that became more complex as it took on practical and diplomatic form. But it would take too long to discuss this problem at the moment.

10. Palanque, *S. Ambroise et l'Empire romane,* pp. 402-403.
11. Cf. Battifol, *Le siège apostolique,* chap. 11.
12. Palanque, *op. cit.,* p. 91.

In any event, reflection on that Council's conclusion would oblige us to notice that there had been a tendency to emancipate the Church from any political interference. But an attempt was still made to preserve a solidarity of thought and action between the princes and the Church. Such reflection would also oblige us to see the Council as going beyond doctrinal affirmations to proclaim disciplinary and moral decrees —vigorously and indefatigably promoted by St. Charles— that will serve later as the foundation for reforming the life of both the clergy and the laity with an efficacy that is still operative in part.[13]

But if all this is worth recalling, it does not change present day reality. It serves only to throw light on the different historical and juridical structures of past ages, and obliges us to note that civil authority, both in Italy and every other state in the world, has nothing to do with the forthcoming Ecumenical Council. Between the Council and modern states there will be neither juridical nor diplomatic nor political relations.

The Unconcern of Secular Society Involves an Incomprehension of the Divine Mystery

Here we see emerge a negative factor that leads to additional considerations. Not every state will be content to remain outside the Church that assembles all its bishops. Some will be opposed to it. Despite the persistent profession of the modern freedoms and despite the incontestable evidence of loyalty that the Catholic Church offers any state that provides it with an opportunity to practice and carry out its spiritual mission, we know that today there still are states that fail to understand, and even deny historical facts of the magnitude and dignity of Christ's Church.

We can however foresee that there will be bishops under

13. Cf. Soranzo, San Carlo, p. 145ff; and Mario Bendiscioli in vol. X of Storia di Milano, p. 134ff.

the rule of communist regimes missing at the Council, if they have survived.

This is not simply a political matter. It is, if you will, a matter that is spiritual or ideological in character. And due to the gravity of this phenomenon, it is no longer the Church's and the Council's external and juridical position in the contemporary world that we are led to consider but rather its moral, ideological and, more properly speaking, religious position. Under this aspect too, at least at first sight, we discern something foreign. Our secular and profane society is instinctively unconcerned with any kind of ecclesiastical manifestation that strikes it as both ritualistic and esoteric. Our world is "In tutt'altre faccende affacendato."[14] In our daily life we do not get excited about religious events of this sort, and when ordinary people do turn their minds to religious matters they think of quite different forms of spiritual expression. They hardly turn their attention to the religious world community that assembles for the purpose of thinking freshly about the Word of Revelation and of legislating in the light of the Holy Spirit.

Yet we would be overlooking some vital aspects of contemporary human reality should we fail to glance, if only in passing, at the profound, unconscious perhaps, though living attitude that our generation bears toward the religious fact, and consequently towards Christ and the Church, the Council's salient expression.

I realize that this is a tremendous, an enormous problem, and so I dare not venture to describe it let alone explore it. But am I mistaken if I should suggest for our present purposes two adjectives that might help us define some of the forms that this general attitude takes: namely, sceptical and demanding?

14. "Wrapped up in totally different matters." The quotation is from Giuseppe Giusti's *Sant'Ambrogio,* familiar to every schoolboy (Trans. Note).

By a sceptic I mean someone who is distrustful and opposed to any kind of transcendence. I mean a man who is turned in upon himself and convinced that reality is confined exclusively within the boundaries of experience—sensible or rational, as may be—boundaries that may perhaps be stretched though they are perpetually controlled by the subjective self. By a sceptic I mean someone who is alone: alone with all the external goods he possesses, knows and enjoys; alone with all his riches, inventions, affairs (for none of these, mute and burdensome, have anything to say to him); alone with his unrest, with the insufficiency of his own thought, with the creeping burden of responsibilities born of his own practical conquests and with a gradual loss of the ability to espouse any kind of value whatsoever, a loss that is born of a paralyzing incertitude. He is alone with his inmost anguish (how fashionable this word has become!) and with the progressive disintegration of every logical and moral norm (are you not familiar with the themes of the contemporary theatre?). He is alone, I say, in perpetual search of himself, and has even lost the capacity of knowing exactly what to think and reason about, just like the subjectivists and agnostics of a former age.

What I have been stressing does seem pessimistic, though it is perhaps less so than certain beliefs of modern man that entail the rapid liquidation of any kind of transcendence. A contemporary writer observes: "This anguish is a first contact, negative to be sure, with all that is essential in reality . . . It is a struggle that aims at abandoning the primacy of thought so as to return to concrete reality . . . While the natural sciences glory in triumph, despair spreads like a drop of oil. A new contact with reality is sought. This fundamental attitude already engenders new philosophical conceptions that are natural to man . . . as they consist in his belief in and reliance on existence in itself."[15]

15. L. C. Baas.

It may well be that a new certitude has yet to be reached after all, though its need has certainly been acknowledged. Modern man needs, craves for a reality that is neither physical alone nor economic, scientific, rational alone, but spiritual as well. And note: I am speaking of reality and not of myth.

The Church's Call to the World

This is the reason why the world looks at the Church in astonishment, for the Church seems to have a wealth of this reality. The world is not altogether deaf to the sound of trumpets which, by convening the Council, greatly honors that reality. Public opinion has been aroused; curiosity has been awakened; open and attentive eyes—such as those of this Institute—have been fixed on the announced event. Thoughtful spirits have begun to meditate about it; men of good will have begun to derive hope from it and rejoice in it.

Spiritually void but anxious, our modern world has by no means been insensitive to the announcement of this event. If nothing else, it has come to realize that the separation which it had been so well brought up to accept—the separation between the Church and secular society—does not exist in the concrete. The Church, the ancient Church, sole survivor of untold shipwrecks in history, does not exist outside the world. On the contrary, it exists in the world, in our world; it exists in our history, in our life. Even more, if we grasp the chief import entailed in the announcement of the Council we realize that the Church exists not only in the world but also for the world. Pius IX had already said that "the Church was born for no other purpose than to make all men share in the redemption, and spread Christ's kingdom throughout the world."[16]

And John XXIII, in an admirable address to the Council's Preparatory Commissions, has said:

16. *A.A.S.*, 1926, 65.

In the modern period the face of the world has changed profoundly and it is hard for it to keep its balance between the attractions and the perils of a constant and almost exclusive pursuit of material goods, and in the midst of a total neglect or watering down of the supernatural, spiritual principles that characterized the implanting and spread of Christian civilization through the centuries. In this modern period, the question is not so much one of some particular point or other of doctrine or of discipline that has to be brought back to the pure fonts of Revelation and of tradition, as it is of restoring the substance of humane and Christian thinking and living (for which the Church has served as custodian and teacher through the centuries) to full force and to its proper splendor.

On the other hand, it is certainly important and even obligatory for us to deplore the errors and faults of a human spirit that is being tempted and pushed in the direction of concentrating completely on enjoyment of the earthly goods that modern scientific research now puts within the easy grasp of the man of our age. But may God keep us from exaggerating the extent of this to the point of making ourselves believe that God's heavens have now closed over our head once and for all, that, as a matter of fact, "darkness has covered the whole earth," and that there is nothing left for us to do but shed tears as we plod along our difficult path.

Instead, we must take courage.[17]

We must therefore conclude that the Council is not only an internal fact in the Church's life but that it also wishes to be, and in fact in some way could be an event for the world, a hope for all.

The Council and Its Relations with the Contemporary World

If this is so, then we should consider two perspectives: one that looks at the forthcoming Council from without, and the other that looks outside, to the world, from within the Church.

I have little to say about the first perspective, and indeed confess that I would rather listen and inquire. I should like

17. *The Pope Speaks,* vol. 6, No. 4 (1960), 378-379.

to know what those who observe the Church expect from the Council. Those among them who are hostile will say nothing, indeed will have no good word whatsoever to say. Those who are indifferent will ask: what on earth can an ecclesiastical event of this sort offer the modern world? Those who are educated, intelligent and informed will entertain a great many suppositions; while simple and good-hearted people will make up fantasies and live in hopes, not without a touch of utopia and some ingenuity. The inquiry has begun and remains open.

A booklet has been published recently in Germany with eighty-one answers to the one question: what do we expect from the Council?[18] And in France another survey has been made among christians of different denominations: "Expectations of the Council."[19] The *Annuario di Politica Internazionale*—one of this Institute's excellent publications—also demonstrates the importance of the forthcoming Council and the interest that it has aroused.

For my part, as I look at the world that awaits the Council, I can simply say that if any contact should be established between the ecclesiastical event and the contemporary world, this contact will not take place in the political sphere. This observation may perchance disappoint professional politicians or those who expect a prophetic flame to spring up from the political scene, or again expect that the Vatican will gather the representatives of nations in order to settle their problems and introduce peace among them. Yet I believe that this observation is justified.

And I do not believe that it underestimates the greatness of the event, for that event finds its proper value in a sphere other than the political. I will go much further and say that perhaps the Council will even fail to remedy the many theoretical errors and moral evils that exist in the world. The Council may identify and proscribe them, and then suggest

18. *Umfrage zum Konzil,* 1961.
19. *Esprit,* December, 1961.

remedies, but it will not be a miracle drug producing an immediate effect, nor will it herald a holy and happy era.

I do not believe that the Council will thunder out anathemas against the world, even though it will be obliged to speak the firm, sharp and clear language of truth. This too will perhaps be something new in the Church's way of conducting its councils, for throughout its history the Church has as a rule exercised its highest authoritative teaching by defending positive truths in a negative and condemning manner. In his great book *de civitate Dei* St. Augustine makes the precise observation that the Church's doctrinal thought has progressed under the stimulus of opposed errors: "A problem raised by an adversary furnishes an opportunity for learning" (16, 2).

The Church will indeed appear majestic and grave, and will stand upright in the face of the world. It will display the spiritual disposition that Pope John XXIII has intended to impress on it in his recent solemn document, *Mater et Magistra.*

Consequently the greatest effort will be made, both within and without the Council, towards a religious affirmation that will entail a rigorous commitment and an unswerving fidelity to the Gospel, to Revelation, to God's Word, to living tradition and the consistent magisterium in which the Council finds its reason for being and the secret of its perpetually youthful longevity. But the outside world will notice certain traits that concern it at the precise moment in which the Church is engaged in an inward renewal of its life.

It will notice a primary, stupendous and over-arching mark, namely the calling of separated christians back to Christ's one Church. It is known that, far more than a characteristic note, this is one of the Ecumenical Council's aims, together with the Church's inner reform and a vigorous and genuine affirmation of the christian religion. This aim, this hope may have been the first spark to enkindle in the Pope's heart the desire to convene the Council. This was an act of loving boldness that is ever the greater and more moving, the more vain and rash (humanly speaking) is the confidence we have that the Council will fully achieve this aim. Yet love is never vain, and trust in Christ never rash.

Should the Council fail to celebrate the return of the separated brothers it will at least succeed in opening the doors and clearing the road to the paternal house, in issuing an affectionate invitation to take them back into the one truly apostolic and Catholic Church. Ecumenism will become the measure of desires, constitutions and prayers, and will be a great event for bringing peace to the world and for acknowledging that spiritual foundation without which union among nations becomes so very difficult and precarious.

Another trait that the world may wish to note is the Church's effort to make its message intelligible so that it—the world—may at least be enabled to listen, in order later to welcome and carry out that message in its concrete life. In its rigorously faithful obedience to Christ's mandate to guard and transmit the sacred *depositum* intact, the Church has swathed it with great solicitude in rites, a language and customs that, as I was saying, serve in part to preserve it untarnished by the ravages of time and the alteration produced by subjective interpretations, and in part must serve to make it clear, intelligible and acceptable to mankind.

Now this vital aim that the apostolic mission has adopted as its own law admits and demands that the religious message, in its authentic content, be adapted to the intelligence and in part also the taste of men who in the course of centuries have changed their language and mental habits. It is a question of cleaning up and restoring the external appearance of religion, of facilitating its circulation through the language, culture and art of our age. And this the Council will do, even if it should defend Latin as a sacerdotal and universal language, even if it should preserve our immortal liturgy in its genuine and marvelous expressions. And there will be more things of interest to our world, I believe.

For not only will the Council endeavor to make our religion intelligible again; it will also endeavor to make it workable. Let no one think that the Church will ever change the laws that God has willed as the foundation and protection of human life. On the contrary, we expect the Church, in the Council itself, to defend its laws with inflexibility.

But there are ecclesiastical laws, and some of these are outdated. They are applicable to the exigencies of modern life only with some difficulty. This is the reason why there is talk of an "aggiornamento" in canon law, which is the only type of legislation (with the exception of the statutes governing the communication services among nations) that has remained until this very day world-wide in scope.

Allow me to add a final observation, still with respect to the Ecumenical Council in its relations with the contemporary world. The Church gathered together in the Council will display another exciting attitude: that of assimilating the secular but human forms of modern life. Though it would take a long time to understand this attitude, a quick survey should be enough to make our thought clear.

We all know how, in the age of the Greco-Roman pagan civilization, the Church rejected whatever idolatrous and inhuman elements it contained while it preserved, purified and assimilated the treasures of classical culture and art. We know how in feudal times it did indeed oppose everything that was barbaric and violent in that historical manifestation of new peoples while it accepted, corrected and ennobled the powers of medieval man. And again, we all know how at the time of the Renaissance the Church curbed the intoxicated forces of a reborn pagan humanism and made its artistic excellence its own by raising it to incomparable heights.

Just as the Church did all this so, I dare believe, it will once again denounce every kind of materialism that is typical of our age. Yet it will never damn our gigantic and wondrous civilization with its science, industry, technology and internationalized life. On the contrary, it will endeavor to "incorporate" our civilization—that is, furnish it, at its roots, with stable and sound principles that it does not yet possess, and at the top open it up to horizons of spiritual truths, prayer and redemption that it alone is truly capable of providing.

The Church will endeavor to accomplish today what it has been in fact accomplishing for centuries: that is to say, it will bring peace and brotherhood to all men by making them God's children in Christ. As always, it will endeavor to bless the world with a soul, a christian soul.

And so we shall see how the Church, in celebrating its Ecumenical Council, will also offer the world a token of trust, friendship and hope.

Councils in the Life
of the Church

Necessity of Studying Some of the Council's Prospects

Much has already been spoken and written about the Ecumenical Council since Pope John XXIII—almost by divine inspiration, we may say (to use the phrase cut into the arch of Constantine, *instinctu divinitatis*)— declared his intention of convening Vatican Council II without any advance public announcements and without any compelling external cause.

We too have spoken about it, at Passo della Mendola. We were invited there by the Catholic University. Forever faithful to its high purposes of thought, it wished then—as it does now—to pay homage through research and writing to a fact that is as fecund as any in its power of illumination, and as worthy of any for profound meditation. Let us therefore pay tribute to this university, even though it is not our words that will really honor it. We have already said something about the Council this year in our pastoral letter, in which we invited our faithful to think of the forthcoming Council in the light of some criteria that will enable them to understand it in a way that is simple and easy as well as certain and profitable.

This simplifies our present lecture, and so we shall restrict ourselves to the topic that the organizers of the university lectures have specified. We shall also limit ourselves to a brief discussion of a council's significance in the Church's life, with special reference to the forthcoming Council.

What does a council represent in the Church's life? This question lends itself to a two-fold answer. We may study the significance that a council assumes inside the Church as well as the significance that it acquires for those who observe it from outside; and then we can compare it with the outside world. We shall confine ourselves to a consideration of the first aspect (that is, a council's importance in the Church's inner life).

We Should Deepen the Concept of "Church"

First of all, it is impossible to have a concept of an ecumenical council without having a concept of the Church. A doctrine about the Church is necessary in order to understand what a council is.

A council is a solemn act, an extraordinary moment, an extremely important event in the Church's life, and so we must know the essence of the Church before we can grasp the importance and nature of a council. Right now a study of the Church would carry us very far. Here we need only advert to the necessity of clarifying and deepening our ideas on the Church before we can possibly understand the nature of a council. At the same time, by doing this we reach a first, fundamental and very fruitful conclusion: a council is a reflective act concerning the nature of the Church. We are all invited to ask: What is the Church?

This eminently simple question immediately creates difficulties if only because of the variety of answers that are possible. It is rather similar to the one, almost maieutic in nature, that Christ asked his disciples at Caesarea Philippi:

"What do men say of the Son of Man? Who do they think he is?" (Mt 16:13). As the Apostles report, the great number of people who accepted the opinions then current about Christ the son of man bespeaks their embarrassment, and shows how difficult it is to formulate a clear and univocal answer about him. For we must wait for Simon—who later was called and became Peter—before we can speak of a clear definition. Moved by an inner revelation, he gave us the famous definition that established an equation—indeed, an identity of persons—between the two revealed natures of Christ: the son of man is the son of God. Christ's mystery blazes forth and blinds.

And so with the Church. What do you say of our Church, the Church that is celebrating this extraordinary event? We find ourselves in the presence of a mystery, and it is well that this is so. What the Council invites us to do is precisely to gain a fresh consciousness of the Church's mystery.

In this way we involve ourselves in the most exciting and living movement of contemporary religious thought, and in the most passionate and advanced theological studies. While in the past the idea of the Church was a matter of experience rather than thought, today it is the very reverse. Yet the experience will certainly be a living one, if it is profoundly meditated. And once again, through a profound and prolonged act of consciousness, the Church will become for itself, and for the world too, what it is and what it ought to be.

Father DeLubac speaks wisely in these words: "From the very start you feel that she has an extraordinarily deep awareness of her own being; the idea of the Church is everywhere, and everywhere shapes the expounding of faith. In addition, at a very early stage she is compelled to begin the process of reflexion on herself. Every one of the great heresies that she has to fight forces this upon her . . . All the mysteries which she examines, one by one, provide occasions for the same thing, for she is bound up with each and finds herself involved in all of them. Yet today we are at the beginning of an attempt at an unfolding which is at once analytic and generalized—an attempt to grasp the mystery in its totality; and circumstances have never before made necessary an effort of this kind."[1] Today it is precisely the Ecumenical Council that furnishes the most favorable and compelling condition for this act of self-understanding on the part of the Church.

And what may astonish and arrest our attention is the following consideration. The consciousness that the Church is anxious to form of itself today is with respect to its inmost, profound and mysterious aspects. It is not a question of those aspects that everybody can easily learn about and observe: its human composition, its canon law, its chronological and actual history, its external manifestations such as its institutions, its presence in the world, its art, and so forth. The Church is eager to explore and to experience the mystery of its own life. It is in search of its own theology, its own soul, its own secret. And it is within itself that it searches for Christ in so far as he dwells with the Holy Spirit. The Church is in search of God's thought, design, presence, action.

It is only through the acts it produces that we can know our soul, so philosophers tell us. In a similar way—with the exception of what divine revelation has already taught us— we can gain no better knowledge of the Church's soul, of its profound life, of its indwelling divine mystery than through experiencing its life, through a consciousness of its powers and activity. Now a council is a supreme act in the Church's life. While it does presuppose a knowledge of the Church itself, it illuminates, develops and celebrates this knowledge through action and reflection.

We therefore expect a council's thought on the Church to be somewhat circular. Before we can accept a council as a legitimate act of the Church we must begin with an outline, at least, of an ecclesiological doctrine. We should always

1. Henri de Lubac, *The Splendour of the Church*, p. 3.

bear in mind, for example, the teachings concerning the plurality and convergence of causes from which the Church derives its life. The efficient cause is God who thinks, wills and arouses the Church through Christ, through the Apostles, and through the hierarchy derived from them. The formal life-giving cause is the Holy Spirit, the Church's uncreated soul who through grace, a created life-giving power, inbreathes life in faith and charity. The material cause is mankind called to form the Church with Adam's poor and perishable clay (though a clay shaped by the love that makes it Christ's bride). The final cause is the mystical body, holy and transfigured, that grows more and more compact in time and that is destined to live in eternity in the perfection and beatitude of the heavenly Church.

Thus, in order that we may gain a better understanding of the humanity that makes up the Church, we shall always keep our minds alert to the human element that today has been called into a happy though still restricted symbiosis with the divine element of our supernatural life. And we shall ask ourselves if this symbiosis, if this divine assistance granted to the Church, might not find some absolutely certain and tangible expression that will overcome our ordinary human frailty, and thereby enable it to become infallibly clear and invincibly strong.

The Council will respond in the affirmative to our bold yearning. The divine element will manifest itself in and through the human element. In the Council men who are of this world will be invested with charismatic powers and will speak through the movement of the Holy Spirit. "It is the Holy Spirit's pleasure and ours . . ." (Acts 15:28): so declared the very first Council of Jerusalem through the words of the Apostles, and so the subsequent councils will speak, with the certainty that they are the instruments of a theandric action. Our concept of the Church's divine-human composition will become a living reality, an outer and inner experience that will triumphantly embody that timid and difficult doctrine, and engender a magnificent joy in it.

The Church's Social Constitution

A council proves and confirms another fundamental point of ecclesiology as it corroborates doctrine with experience, for doctrine is founded on experience: in this case, the Church's social constitution.

Let us proceed by way of simple examples. We already know that the Church is a visible and hierarchical society. It is not a simple religious phenomenon, nor is it a simple faith that reaches out to an indefinite range of minds, thereby creating an invisible ideal bond among them, as in the case of doctrines and opinions of human thought. Nor is it even the resulting community of believers, that makes itself visible and concrete through a certain uniformity in accepting a word which—by what authority nobody knows—is said to be divine. The Church is born of the Apostles' initiative, of an authority that derives its mandate from Christ and creates a community around it that is visible, organized and governed.

We surely know who Peter is and who the Apostles are, and we also know who succeeds the former and who the latter. We know everything about their authority and their mission. We know how the Pope's magisterium and jurisdiction, in their mysterious range, make the pontifical keys both necessary and sufficient for governing the Church; and we likewise know that the powers of the apostolic college are subordinate and coessential with respect to those of the Church's head. But the moment that the Church gives us not only the conceptual scheme of this marvellous constitution of the Church but also its living action—its bodily functioning, I might say—then our wonder will increase, our understanding of the Church's sovereign laws will become vision, our knowledge will rejoice. We shall then see in the

Church thus operative (and reflected with absolute fidelity) the constitutive principles that the divine founder and architect, Christ the Lord, has proclaimed for the building of his Church.

The Council will bring out into plain view the Church's social, visible, organized, hierarchical, episcopal and pontifical aspect. It will be an apologia in action of the doctrine about the council that is already familiar to us. It is indeed known that the desire to see the forthcoming Council reflect this doctrinal design as faithfully and completely as possible has prompted many people to hope that Vatican Council II will integrate the doctrinal teachings on the Church's constitution that Vatican Council I proclaimed only in part.

And let us note that it is not only the Council fathers but all of us who are invited to deepen our consciousness of the Church's nature and mystery. And so, through this extraordinary event, every child of the Church is urged to meditate freshly on what the encyclical on the mystical body has already exhorted us to do: "nothing can be imagined more glorious, undoubtedly nothing more honorable, than to belong to the holy Catholic apostolic Roman Church. Through it we become members of one sole and venerable body, and are guided by one sole and thus supreme head, are filled with one sole and divine Spirit . . ."[2]

A council is an extraordinary occasion and a powerful stimulus for increasing "the sense of the Church" throughout the whole Catholic world. Romano Guardini's memorable words seem to have been uttered for this occasion: "A religious process of incalculable importance has begun—the Church is coming to life in the souls of men."[3]

This seems even more obvious, right and proper if we relate it to an ecumenical council. We must consider that

2. *A.A.S.*, 1943, p. 237.
3. Romano Guardini, *The Church and the Catholic and the Spirit of the Liturgy* (New York: Sheed and Ward, 1935), p. 11.

although a council does express the faith of the whole Church, it does this not because the bishops have been so delegated by the faithful; it rather does so because the bishops are witnesses and teachers of the Church's common faith. They share directly in the religious life of the entire community of believers who defend the deposit of faith. In this respect we might recall Newman's famous words about whether or not the faithful should be consulted in matters of doctrine. He meant this not in so far as they are a normative source of faith, but in so far as they are a sign of the religious belief that normally and rightly pervades christian people.[4] Whence we can see the two-fold aim of a council: to arouse a consciousness of the Church within the Catholic world; to obtain from that world—especially as it prepares itself for the sessions—presentations of its teaching that it will judge later as to the authenticity of their christian value.

In a recent pastoral letter on "the meaning of a council" (which they define as an inner reform of Catholic life), the Dutch bishops assert that "conciliar decisions and decrees are the powerful manifestation of an active collaboration, in matters of faith, of the whole community of believers: the pope, the bishops, priests and laymen accompanied by the judgment of the hierarchy that, moved by the Spirit, examines, defines and corrects everything."[5]

The Characteristic Notes of the Church Expressed by a Council

These considerations lead us to observe a fresh and even more evident aspect that an ecumenical council assumes in the Church's life. A council is not only an act whereby the Church becomes conscious of itself. It is also, and even more

---

4. J. H. Newman, *Pensée sur l'Église*, pp. 402ff; 434, 19; J. Hamer, "Le Concile Oecumenique," *Lumière et Vie*, 62ff.
5. Hamer, *op. cit.*, p. 41.

so, an act whereby it declares the fullness of its being and its operative powers. An ecumenical council mobilizes the whole Church and lifts it to its full stature, its utmost efficiency, its total capacity for prayer, doctrine, government, inner reform, missionary tension, eschatological hope. It activates a sanctity that flows in as well as a sanctity that flows out. And so it is not surprising that its external appearance should bring out the full splendor of its distinctive and characteristic notes in such a way as to make of the Church —both for its own members and for those honestly observing it from the outside—a sign, a proof, a confirmation of divine revelation realized and incarnated in mankind.

The Church's apostolic note is clearly embodied in the protagonists of a council: the pope and the bishops. Their meeting brings out in the clearest light the consistent, uninterrupted and faithful derivation of the instrumental function of the hierarchy in the Church that goes back to the Apostles, to Christ, to God. Christ's words take on flesh before our very eyes: "I came upon an errand from my Father, and now I am sending you out in my turn" (Jn 20:21). "Thou hast sent me into the world on thy errand, and I have sent them into the world on my errand . . . It is not only for them that I pray; I pray for those who are to find faith in me through their word" (Jn 17:18, 20).

The mystical reality of the episcopacy, etched in the admirable words of the bishop of Antioch martyred in Rome towards the beginning of the second century, coincides with the juridical structure that the Apostles' successors have assumed in the Church: "Be subject to the bishop and let this be mutual, as Christ was subject to the Father according to the flesh, and the Apostles to Christ, to the Father and to the Spirit so that the union might be physical as well as spiritual" (*ad Magnesios*, 13,2). Assembled in a council in its full force, the Church manifests its apostolic nature both through the form and mark conferred upon it by the presence of the episcopal body derived from the apostolic college and through the causal action which the bishops have exercised in it since the time of the Apostles.[6]

The same may be said of the Church's unity that a council manifests with an impressive splendor due to the position the pope assumes in it. For there is no place like the council, let us note, in which the pope is so clearly head, center and corner-stone. It is precisely so that it may respond to the essential need of unity that the Church does acknowledge and celebrate as both providential and divine the sovereign privileges of necessity and sufficiency that Christ has furnished his vicar for teaching and governing the whole Church. The Church also manifests its unity as the whole world converges around Peter's successor.

A council offers us a vision of the Catholic world become one with a clarity that seems dim to our modern anxious desire to see reality expressed in phenomenal aspects. In a council the whole Catholic world is present through its bishops. The Church's universality is clearly shown by the bishops' numbers and place of origin as well as by their language, race, culture and history. And if we observe well we shall notice that this concourse of representative men is not purely accidental and fortuitous. It is not promoted by purely juridical bonds or by particular interests aiming to resolve their differences, as might be the case with the great civil international organizations. Much less does this concourse come about and persist through a mortifying levelling of those distinctive traits that every people stamps on its children. On the contrary, it is a profound and spiritual catholic unity engendered by the identity of faith and charity (that is, of the most personal and living expressions of the human spirit). Through a mysterious and marvellous divine combination this faith and this charity find themselves united into a single rigorous and fraternal respect for every single person and an

6. Charles Journet, *op. cit.*, I, pp. 526ff.

harmonious happiness of all. It is the Catholic world manifest-
ing the reality and fullness of its communion; it is the Church
celebrating both its unity and its catholicity.

And so we see a truly ecumenical encounter, at last perfect,
at last universal by right, and to a very large extent also in
fact. We see the universality of Christ's true Church con-
summated at last in faith and love.

And what about sanctity, the final characteristic of the
Church, that should be the most beautiful and most desired?
Will sanctity also be manifested in a council? For those who
believe, for those who know how to see the reality of grace,
sanctity too will send forth wondrous rays from a council's
ecclesial plentitude. For we know, as Christ has promised,
that where the Apostles are gathered in his name, there is he
himself in their midst. And we know that the Holy Spirit's
assistance is never so fully invoked and never so complete as
it is when the teaching Church gathers to speak in his name.
But beyond this supernatural sanctity a council gives evidence
of another kind. There is a moral sanctity that it wishes to
point out and arouse in the Church in a variety of ways.
Through its legislation and through a reform of thought and
life it is aiming to introduce this moral sanctity among the
clergy and the laity with a wisdom never before so thoroughly
meditated, with disposition never before so authoritative,
with measures and suggestions never before so efficacious.

In a council the Church is in a state of tension. This in
itself is a sign of a mature judgment and will that it first produces in the responsible hierarchy, and then undertakes to
transmit to the body of priests, religious and laymen.

In this respect a council is a search for the authentic faith
and morals that Christ has willed, a release from the corro-
sive and perishable sediment that, throughout the years and
amidst the vicissitudes of this world, has settled on the immaculate garments of Christ's spouse. A council is a source
of fresh energies: at first dormant in the heart of the Church,

they are later propagated among men so that they may be inundated with grace and a renewed will.

These are the fruits that an ecumenical council produces. Vatican Council I has asserted them in the following words: "There it is that the sacred dogmas of religion are defined with the greatest depth, expressed with the greatest breadth, that ecclesiastical discipline is restored and more firmly established . . . that head and members are knit together and the vigour of the whole Mystical Body of Christ renewed . . . that our zeal is nourished to extend, even were it with our blood, the reign of Christ over all the earth."[7]

A Council Gives the Church's Countenance a Full and Radiant Expression

But perhaps the fullness that a council bestows on the Church's external countenance involves additional specific effects engendered by this extraordinary act of its life? That it does so is indeed common knowledge, for an ecumenical council provokes a moment of intense clarity in ecclesiastical consciousness. It not only lifts the current manifestation of the Church's life to a moment of experienced and demonstrable, visible fullness; it also marks an extraordinary moment of action. It is the supreme and operative organ of authority in the whole Church.[8] Thus it may best be described as that moment in the Church's life which displays its powers in their highest degree, with special emphasis on two in particular: the power of the magisterium and the power of jurisdiction. In an ecumenical council the Church becomes an eminently efficient teacher: it becomes queen.

In a council Christ's powers become active in a supreme form and measure. Authoritarian though he was, St. Charles defended council and synod on many an occasion and gave

7. The Constitution *Dei Filius*, quoted by Journet, *ibid.*, p. 418.
8. Canon 228, 1.

proof of his belief through his pastoral action. In fact it is in this respect that he usually considers an ecumenical council as both providential and necessary. For the moment I shall not consider what sort of relationship holds between the pontifical power and the power of the episcopal college. I shall only observe that the pontifical power is acknowledged to be, even in itself, infallible in teaching and sovereign in its pastoral jurisdiction. In order to enjoy those same privileges, the power of the episcopal college must be in communion with the pope who must convene, preside over and validate it, just as the members of a body, in order to live and function, must be joined to that body's head. I shall not dwell on this point since it too is well known to everybody, especially since Vatican Council I has issued its mandatory definitions on these points of ecclesiastical constitutional law and of the theology of the Church's mystery.

I am saying something rather different: namely, that supreme conciliar powers have been exercised for different reasons, which means that special circumstances and needs have called forth the intervention of the ecumenical council's authority. And this amounts to saying that ecumenical councils have a history. Indeed, it is they above all that make up the history of the Church. It is in councils that the Church lives its principal events and its decisive moments, and in councils that its experiences are manifested in distinctive and determinative ways, its dramas most laborious and triumphant.

On this subject I recall an incident with regard to Giacinto Gaggia, who was a great bishop and a man of very wide culture, a man of great genius no less than great will. It is to him that I owe many good offices, and especially my ordination to the priesthood. I was a very young priest at the time, and was already thinking of studying the life of the Church. I consulted him—in a shy and hesitant manner—as to what books I should read in organizing my studies. He immediately replied: "Go and read the history of the councils. Get hold of Hefele [18 heavy volumes!] and study them, for in them you can find everything," namely, theology, philosophy, spirituality, politics, humanism and christianity, errors, debates, truths, abuses, laws, virtues and the Church's sanctity. The history of the councils is an ecclesiastical encyclopedia. And this in itself demonstrates the place that councils hold in the Church's life: they pervade it completely and sum it up; they illuminate and guide it.

The councils are the great poles on which is strung the historical cable of the living Church; they are the milestones of its age-old journey.

A Glance at Past Councils

And here we can easily see the opening up of the past centuries that have been marked by twenty-two ecumenical councils (or twenty-one, according to conflicting criteria of calculation), and here we can easily be induced to note what functions these solemn and troubled assemblies have actually carried out. But we shall refrain from doing this. It would be easy to classify the ecumenical councils according to the specific purposes for which they were convened. The first councils, for example, are specifically doctrinal in character: Nicea, Constantinople, Ephesus, Chalcedon; and so were the four following councils, all celebrated in the East.

Then come the ecumenical councils that took place in the West and are characterized by the medieval controversies involving the conflict between the two swords, the ecclesiastical and the civil. These councils are chiefly juridical in nature, and aim at the freedom of the Church. Then the problem of reestablishing unity occupies the following councils, up to the very difficult councils of Constance, Basle, Ferrara and Florence. Finally at Trent there is the great council of the Church's dogmatic and disciplinary restoration that has left such a great mark on the Church's life up to, we may well say, our very own day. (We should be especially grateful to our own St. Charles who worked so diligently to put the Council's decrees into practice.)

The Tridentine council is assigned an important and pre-eminent place in the Church's life by the distinguished historian of the seventeenth century, Cardinal Sforza Pallavicino: "No council lasted a longer time, none was broader for the number of articles of faith decided, none more efficacious in changing life and laws, none more arduous for obstacles encountered, none more exact in diligence in examining the problems at hand. Finally—as invariably happens in all great works—none was exalted more by friends nor vituperated more by enemies."[9]

And von Pastor concludes his treatment of the Council of Trent in the following words: "To sum up, it is difficult to estimate too highly the importance of the Council of Trent, especially for the interior development of the Church. It laid the foundations of a true reform, and fixed Catholic doctrine on broad and systematic lines. It is at once a boundary line and a landmark, at which opposing spirits must separate, and it inaugurates a new epoch in the history of the Catholic Church."[10]

Even those who find a great many imperfections in the Council of Trent, chiefly because of the historical circumstances and customs of the time, must acknowledge the salutary and capital importance of that council.[11] But if the Council of Trent did save the Church at that time, it did not recover what the Protestant Reformation had taken away: people and provinces. "The Church had recovered from the

9. Cardinal Sforza Pallavicino, *Storia . . .*, I, 2.
10. Ludwig von Pastor, *The History of the Popes,* edited by R. F. Kerr (London: Kegan Paul, Trench, Trubner and Co., Ltd., 1928), vol. XV, p. 378.
11. Dupont, "Le Concile de Trent," *Le Concile et les Conciles* (Paris: Ed. de Cerf, 1960), pp. 281ff.

crisis of the sixteenth century," Murphy writes, "but it was not able to undo the evil wrought by the Revolt. The sad remembrances are still with us today."[12]

And so, three hundred years later, Vatican Council I resumed the work. The men who burst forth from the great Protestant crisis invaded the world and dramatically stamped their image on the human culture that on the one hand was triumphantly moving towards the mathematical and physical sciences, and on the other was negatively engaged in corroding and dissolving the validity not only of traditional faith but of thought as well. And it did the latter so well that it impregnated thought with a subjectivism and a self-sufficiency that in turn was immediately overcome by systematic doubt and feeble forms of idealism.

The Church's magisterium had to resume its mission in order to consolidate the laws and natural powers of thought, and finally advance a constitutional definition of the Church. These are vital themes that were in fact first embodied in the dogmatic propositions discussed with such great animation at Vatican Council I.

Since the last century, we may say, the Church has found in these conclusions a platform for shaping its life and pursuing its struggle. It is enough to recall the formidable development in the last century of the Church's didactic and functional aims, for these aims have been made sacred and fruitful by the definition of papal infallibility in certain authorized and solemn acts of the pope's magisterium. But as we all know, Vatican Council I was interrupted, and though the whole Church certainly knew that its teachings were incomplete, nobody knew if and when and how the Church's conciliar function would be resumed. There were even some, both within and without the Church, who doubted the use-

12. John L. Murphy, *The General Councils of the Church* (Milwaukee: Bruce, 1960), p. 169.

fulness of the council as an institution, since it was acknowledged that the pope had the powers of a sovereign government and of an infallible magisterium, even without the support of a council.

The fact that Vatican Council II has been convened through the free and spontaneous initiative of the Pope himself, dispels this doubt and proves that the permanent activity of these universal assemblies of the Church's teaching and governing body that we call ecumenical councils are permanently active.

What Significance Will Vatican Council II Have?

For us one last and extremely interesting question remains to be answered before we conclude this brief and elementary outline of our assigned theme: namely, what significance does the forthcoming Council assume in the Church's life? And even more: what significance will it have? Many people have already tried to answer these questions either by advancing acute evaluations about the present state of the Church and the world, or by allowing themselves both the pleasure and the risk of engaging in predictions. Some find easy suggestions in the unfinished program of Vatican Council I. They believe that a definition of the episcopal function requires the attention of the forthcoming Council: with how many and what kind of repercussions in the Church's life it is easy to imagine. Some, on the other hand, look at the Church in the light of historical conditions, and would therefore like the Council to resolve—unfortunately it will not be able to do this—or at least prepare a solution of the age-old problem of the separation among christians, a problem that has become so burdensome as to seem unbearable. And so the Church's unity turns out to be a compelling necessity, an over-arching exigency, an inescapable problem. This problem undoubtedly finds its most appropriate setting in a council, and at the same time demonstrates the great importance of a council in the Church's life.

The grandeur and scope of this problem are such as to arouse the interest of the whole christian people. And if it can be treated and resolved in such a competent place as the conciliar sessions, it can and must find in the consciousness of all christians, and especially of Catholics, its proper understanding, suffering and psychological preparation as well as its spiritual and social expression. Once again we can see clearly the relationship, on a vast and complex scale, between a council and the Church's life.

And then there are those who look at the Church's moral and disciplinary situation, and immediately find in it hopes and programs for the forthcoming Council. In this respect one desire does stand out, one that is ardent in the Church's most devout and active children: the desire for a more rigorous and more direct penetration of the spirit of the Gospel into the Church's spiritual and practical life. Whence the proposals for what we may call the inner reform of its life. We must, these zealous people say, cultivate more profoundly and propagate more widely God's word, Holy Scripture. We must make the liturgy a prayer that is alive, so that it may not only be understood and followed by the faithful but may also engender in them a sense and taste of the community as it prays and celebrates the mystery of Christ's perennial presence in his Church. We must "strengthen spiritual values" (Voillaume), make of the forthcoming council an apostolic message, and bestow upon the life of christians the efficacy of those eloquent signs that are known as poverty, love, and contemplative prayer.

After considering the problem of inner reform, many people turn to the attitude that the Church and christian life must assume with respect to the external world. We are referring to the reforms known as "aggiornamento" both in the manner of presenting Catholic thought and in the practical and contingent ways of establishing contact with contemporary society. The Church, they say, must be neither exclusivistic nor anachronistic. On the contrary, it must immerse itself in the historical experience of peoples, assume those forms of life that are sound, and consequently acceptable, and engender fresh forces, as it has done so many times in the past.

The Council must indicate the general line of christian relativism; it must indicate, that is to say, up to what point the Catholic religion must be a rigorous custodian of absolute values, and up to what point it may and should yield to a connatural approach to human life as it is actually lived in the historical concrete. This is a delicate and difficult task that only the wisdom and authority of the teaching Church, and even more of the Council, can carry out.

In a lecture, "Vatican Council II in the Face of Contemporary Thought," Cardinal Frings states exactly that one of the most significant aspects and one of the most relevant tasks that the forthcoming Council must consider is that of "opening the Church, even more than has been done up till now, to that great variety of the human spirit that is its right precisely in so far as it is Catholic."

What shall we say? What significance will the forthcoming Council have in the Church's life?

For our part, we dare advance no precise prognostication. We shall simply say that one forecast does seem certain to us, and is in fact shared by everybody since the Pope himself has proposed it. The forthcoming Council will bring new life to the Church and will be a new spring, a taste of that "second spring" in which Newman discovered a sign of the Church's divine vitality. It will be a renewal of consciousness and energy, a certitude of faith and a wealth of charity, an apostolic impulse and a capacity for heroism and holiness. And all this will bear witness to both the Church and an honest and hospitable world, that the words which Christ addressed to it before leaving this world in the body are actually and perennially true: "And behold I am with you all through the days that are coming, until the consummation of the world" (Mt 28:20).

BIBLIOGRAPHICAL NOTE

La Chiesa (1957–1962) was published in 1962 by the archdiocesan press of Milan as a volume in its series of *Discorsi dell' Arcivescovo di Milano*. "La Chiesa nei suoi aspetti essenziali" was a radio address to the Mission of Milan, 1957; "La missione della Chiesa" was addressed to the 2nd World Congress of the Lay Apostolate, Rome, October, 1957; "La carità della Chiesa verso i lontani" to the 8th National Week of Pastoral Aggiornamento, Milan, September, 1958; "Il segreto della Cattedrale" was delivered on the restoration of the cathedral of Crema, April 26, 1959; "Unità e Papato nella Chiesa" was addressed to the Course of Christian Studies organized by the "Pro Civitate Christiana," Assisi, August 29, 1960; "Ciò che la Chiesa è e non è" to the Mission of Florence, November 10, 1960; "I Concilii Ecumenici nella vita della Chiesa" to the 32nd Course of Cultural Aggiornamento, Passo della Mendola, August 16, 1960; "Pensiamo al Concilio" was his pastoral letter to the Archdiocese of Milan for Lent, 1962; "Il Concilio Ecumenico nel quadro storico internazionale" was addressed to the Institute for the Study of International Politics, April 27, 1962; "I Concilii nella vita della Chiesa" to the University of the Sacred Heart, Milan, 1962.